RESTORING THE VOW OF STABILITY

RESTORING THE VOW OF STABILITY

The Keys to Pastoral Longevity

Richard W. Brown

CHRISTIAN PUBLICATIONS
CAMP HILL, PENNSYLVANIA

Christian Publications
3825 Hartzdale Drive, Camp Hill, PA 17011

The mark of ✝ *vibrant faith*

ISBN: 0-87509-532-1
LOC Catalog Card Number: 93-70741
© 1993 by Christian Publications
All rights reserved
Printed in the United States of America

93 94 95 96 97 5 4 3 2 1

Cover Design: Step One Design

Christian Publications would like to thank the following for use of copyrighted materials:

Quote on pages 219–221 reprinted from *New Visions for the Long Pastorate* by Roy Oswald. Used by permission from The Alban Institute, Inc. 4125 Nebraska Avenue, NW, Washington, DC 20016, Copyright 1983. All rights reserved.

Quote on pages 169–170 taken from *Preaching with Freshness* by Bruce Mawhinney. Copyright © 1991 by Harvest House Publishers, Eugene, OR 97402. Used by permission.

Dedication

To my wife, Kathy:
Thank you for taking our
marital "vow of stability"
so seriously;

and

To the memory
of my mother,
Marion Brown:
Thank you for fulfilling
your responsibility of mothering
so faithfully.

• CONTENTS •

THE VOW

The Dark Ages. Do you know why they called them that? Because there were so many "knights"!

There were also a lot of monks. A lot of restless monks.

Historians tell us that by the sixth century the church was filled with monks on the move. These brown-robed clergy were spiritual individualists on a search for the best in holy living, which gave them a tendency toward wanderlust. It was not unusual for a monk to jump from monastery to monastery, looking for a greater challenge or a more austere holiness. When one place of ministry proved less than ideal, he just went to another—one with a "holier" abbot or "more righteous" companions. He thought if he could find the right community, he would have a more effective ministry and a deeper spiritual life.

It was St. Benedict who finally put a stop to all this restlessness. To the standard vows of poverty, chastity and obedience, he added a fourth—a vow of stability. He called upon the monks to "stay where you are."

THE RESTLESS ONES

Today we have a different name for the problem St. Benedict

1

tried to address. We call it pastoral longevity—the length of time a pastor stays in one church. And it doesn't seem that the clergymen of today are any less restless than they were in the days of old St. Benedict.

Frequently a pastor explains his decision to move on with a mystical announcement such as, "I feel the Lord has called me to a new place of service." While that statement may sound very spiritual, it is often used to hide the real reasons behind the move—reasons neither the pastor nor the congregation fully understand or are willing to discuss.

Meanwhile, everyone knows (but no one wants to admit) that the North American church has developed a pattern of short-term pastorates. And neither pastors nor congregations really understand why. For the time being, at least, it seems that St. Benedict's vow of stability has been forgotten.

A MODERN MONK?

At age 30, Eugene Peterson began his pastorate at Christ Our King Presbyterian Church in Bel Air, Maryland. He had already been inducted into the "pastoral career system," which instructed him to get career counseling, work out career patterns and climb the career ladder. By his own admission, this system struck him at the time as glaringly immature.

But he had also been reading St. Benedict and had been impressed with the wisdom of the monk's radical innovation of the vow of stability. Though the Bel Air church was at that time only a low rung on the pastoral-career ladder, young Eugene determined to stay at Christ Our King for his entire ministry. In 1962 he accepted a self-imposed vow of stability.

In a 1990 *Leadership* magazine article entitled "The Jonah Syndrome," Peterson confessed,

I wish I could boast of keeping my vow of stability, but I cannot. Three times I broke it. Three times in the past twenty-seven years I have gone to the travel agent in Joppa and purchased a ticket for Tarshish. Each of these times I had come to a place where I didn't think I could last another week. I was bored. I was depressed. There was no challenge left, no stimulus to do my best. Spiritually I was in a bog. . . . Preaching to these people was like talking to my dog. . . . The direction of my life was meaningless. . . . I was certain that I was with the wrong congregation.

So I decided to leave for Tarshish. I read the travel folders (in my denomination they are called Church Information Forms). I bought my ticket (this is called "activating your dossier"). I wasn't denying my calling to be a pastor, but I respectfully asserted my right to determine the locale.

I did that three times. Each time, I gave up and went back to the work to which I had already been assigned, to Nineveh. I never did get to Tarshish, but I can take no credit. I tried.[1]

Peterson goes on to admit that there are times when a pastor should move, but he contends that "the norm for pastoral work is stability. Far too many pastors change parishes out of adolescent boredom, not as a consequence of mature wisdom. When this happens, neither pastors nor congregations have access to the conditions that are hospitable to maturing faith."

WHOSE STABILITY IS IT, ANYWAY?

Today's pastors and churches need to think about taking a modern vow of stability. They need to consider the advantages—both to the pastor and to the church—of staying longer.

In the midst of a life filled with change and instability, people today are looking for stability, and one of the places they are looking for it is in the church. Church analyst Lyle Schaller observes that "baby boomers are attracted to congregations that offer the stability and relational advantages provided by a long pastorate."[2] It seems that pastors who take the vow of stability have the opportunity to meet one of the greatest needs of a changing secular society.

Church people are looking for stability, too. After observing the longevity patterns in his city, Pastor John Stevens of the First Presbyterian Church in Colorado Springs, Colorado, wrote: "Pastors move too often. . . . Many pastors . . . sit loose in the saddle because they don't expect to stay too long. . . . [Congregations] tire of bouncing back and forth between pastors and visions of what the church should be. It is difficult for a church like that to develop a consistent approach to ministry."[3]

Schaller identifies a lack of pastoral longevity as one of the major causes of congregational instability, especially in young churches. He notes that a church which has several pastors in its first two decades of existence sets a pattern that usually leads to "arrested development problems." Schaller says that a frequent change in pastors tends to interrupt or divert the process of ministry development and causes many church members to drop into inactivity.[4] Church people seeking stability also need pastors willing to take the vow.

Not only are laypeople looking for stability, so are pastors. A *Leadership* study a few years ago isolated the factors that increase the chances of emotional problems for pastors. One of the troubling factors contributing to the emotional stress of pastors was the short length of time they had been in their current pastorate. The "at-three-to-five-years" discouragement, according to many pastors, comes not only in their first church, but in each church thereafter.[5] And given the fact that the average length of the American pastorate is 3-5 years, short-term pastorates seem to perpetuate instability and stress in the pastor's life.

Add to this the observation of Pastor Juan Ortiz that each time a pastor moves from one church to another, his authority diminishes and that of the local church elders increases. Eventually, Ortiz argues, it reaches a point where the pastor becomes a hireling.[6] When this happens, you can bet that it is anything but a stabilizing environment for either the pastor or the church.

By contrast, a common thread running through the testimonies of pastors of churches that have established a reputation for excellence, stability and growth, is that these pastors have sensed a lifetime call to that church.[7] Research at the Institute for American Church Growth has found that the average tenure for pastors in the largest churches is 21 years.[8] It seems that pastors who have taken a vow of stability have a better chance of producing stable churches.

Darius Salter, in a study conducted for his book *What Really Matters in Ministry*, concluded that successful pastors put down roots in a community. Salter also found that 82 percent of these pastors symbolically communicated that sense of stability to their congregations by purchasing their own home. By such an act the pastor was saying to his church, "I am here to make this my permanent home. I am not looking for greener pastures or for a better appointment. I belong to you and you belong to me."[9]

I believe that more than ever before we need stable pastorates and stable churches. We need pastors and churches who are willing to learn and understand what it means and what it takes to embrace the vow of stability. While the modern-day vow of stability usually will not mean the same as St. Benedict's "stay where you are," it most certainly will mean "stay *longer* where you are."

OUR VERY OWN DARK AGES

How much do we know about the dynamics involved in making longer pastorates possible? Too often mystery surrounds our understanding about how long a modern monk stays and when it is time for him to move. The mystique is reflected in comments like this one from a layperson: "God sends men and He moves them." Or this one from a pastor: "The pastor should ask, 'Is the cloud moving on?'." When it comes to pastors staying longer where they are, it appears as if we are in the "Dark Ages" ourselves.

Surprisingly, not as much has been written on pastoral longevity as you might think. Aside from the published studies listed in the bibliography at the back of this book, *Leadership* has produced the greatest amount of material on the subject. Since its first issue on 1980, this publication has addressed pastoral longevity directly or indirectly in over 40 articles. One entire issue was devoted to "pastoral transitions"; another issue featured articles dealing with "energy and endurance." Just the titles of some of the articles give insight into what is involved in the pursuit of pastoral longevity:

> *Building Trust Between Pastor and Congregation*
> *Hanging on for the Eighth Year*
> *Recycling Pastors*
> *Ministerial Burn-out*
> *Trust—A Crucial Ingredient for Survival*
> *Helping Your Successor Succeed*
> *Romancing the Congregation*
> *Have I Come to the Wrong Church?*
> *Feelings of Failure*
> *Growing Pains*

It is my desire in this book to increase the awareness among pastors, congregations and denominational leadership of the concerns and benefits of pastors staying longer. I also hope to encourage further study on the various aspects of this issue.

WHAT THIS BOOK IS, WHAT IT ISN'T

This book is about identifying things that denominational leaders, educators, pastors and churches are currently doing (or not doing) that get in the way of pastors staying longer. But there are some things that this book is not about:

The pastor's sense of call to ministry. While this subject is vital to a man's ministry and will affect his *career* longevity, it is not directly related to his longevity in a particular pastorate.

The pastor's skills in ministry. Obviously a pastor's proficiency in the areas of preaching, counseling, teaching, visiting, etc., are crucial to his ministry, but these issues are less directly related to longevity in a particular church than are the issues addressed in the chapters to follow.

The pastor's overall theology of the church. A clear understanding of ecclesiology and the biblical role of the pastor by both pastor and people will enhance the possibilities of longevity. Only some of this understanding, however, is directly related to longevity patterns. The theology of ministry that is relevant to pastoral longevity is discussed in chapters five and six.

The pastor's personhood. While a lack of personal growth is listed as an obstacle to longevity, the larger question of the pastor as a person is not addressed. There is, however, a brief mention in chapter four of the leadership styles thought to be most conducive to longevity.

"He got it into his head that he could lower his cholesterol more easily at another church."

While these issues are important for pastors and church people alike, I will not try to address or develop them here. In general, this book is concerned with factors that contribute directly to patterns of short-term or long-term ministries.

For some, pastoral longevity might be an unfamiliar and undefined term. For reasons that will become clearer as you read further, I define a "short-term pastorate" as one that is less than *five* years. I define a "short-term church" as a church that has had at least *three* consecutive pastorates of *four* years or less. I define a "long-term pastorate" as one that lasts at least *nine* years, and a "long-term church" as a church with at least one long-term pastorate in its recent past.

In chapter one, you will read about the need for longer pastorates. Chapters two through four are concerned with the question of value. Statistics may have shown the need for longer pastorates, but who says that longer pastorates are better? These three chapters discuss the pros and cons of longevity.

Chapters five and six take a look at biblical principles and models of longevity in ministry. Chapters seven and eight draw from my interviews with pastors and lay people to develop a list of obstacles to longevity. Read carefully. While many obstacles to *effective ministry* could be listed, only those directly related to *longevity* are addressed.

The final two chapters match the obstacles to longevity with resources for managing those obstacles. Please note that I said managing, not eliminating. This is an admission of the stubborn realities of ministry such as finances, conflicts, mismatches, etc., and an honest conclusion that, though a lifetime pastorate may be an ideal, it is also idealistic. What we need is a more realistic goal in the area of pastoral longevity and a more effective way of attaining that goal.

I have included in the appendices some very helpful material that did not fit comfortably into the main discussion:

Appendix A is the summary statement developed from my study of short-term and long-term pastors and churches. While some of the conclusions noted in the summary statement are discussed in the main chapters, there are a number of other insights that may interest you as you study the issues of pastoral longevity.

Appendix B is a listing of passages in the New Testament that have implications for the issue of pastoral longevity. While the intent of the biblical authors was not to talk about the restless pastor, the passages do suggest some application to the questions we will be asking in this book.

Appendix C is a discussion of the *Myers-Briggs Type Indicator* in identifying the tendencies in a person to be a short-term or a long-term pastor. Let me hasten to add, however, that understanding your natural tendencies does not excuse you from dealing with a short-term pattern. On the contrary, the purpose of learning your personal style is to reach beyond your natural comfort zone, and work on staying longer where you are, for the sake of those to whom you minister.

ON THE PERSONAL SIDE

I started noticing the pattern of restless pastors when I entered the ministry after college. From regular attendance at pastors' conferences, annual denomination councils and a bi-monthly reading of the "Pastoral Transfers" column in our denominational magazine, I came to the realization that pastors were doing a lot of moving around.

Having grown up in two churches whose pastors had both served for 10 or more years, I had personally experienced the benefits of long-term ministries. I had also seen the positive effects of a long-term ministry on my churches and my pastors.

So when I was approaching the end of my seminary education, while pastoring in a rural Wisconsin church, I decided that a long-term pastorate was desirable. I began to consider where God would place me for a long-term ministry. At this stage in my understanding of longevity, I thought that it was ideal for a pastor to stay in one church for a lifetime.

One reason I wanted to commit myself for a lifetime in one church was my tendency to enjoy change. Without such a commitment, I knew that I could easily move from church to church and from new challenge to new challenge after short stays in each place. Long before I was aware of the Myers-Briggs Type Indicator, which helps distinguish personality types as they relate to longevity, I knew that this tendency toward change was a weakness which would hinder my ability to minister to people in-depth. So I set for myself the lifetime commitment—the vow of stability—as a structure within which I would be forced to develop personal relationships and personal ministry skills.

After several months of looking for pastoral opportunities, my wife and I accepted a call from a church in Virginia. We moved in, planning to be there for a lifetime unless God moved us with a crowbar.

Even in those first few years of ministry, I enjoyed some of the benefits of a long-term pastorate. My long-term view gave me patience to work with people. Because I was committed for a lifetime, I could afford the time to wait for them to change. It also had a positive affect on my family life. My wife and I purchased a home and gave birth to three of our four children there. We were settling in to make this place our permanent home.

But in my seventh year of ministry in Virginia, I began to wrestle with offers to candidate at other churches. I use the word "wrestle" because I would literally shake while holding a letter from another church in my hand. These offers frightened me. Later I would come to understand that they represented a threat to my lifetime commitment to the church in Virginia. But what if God wanted me to move? Then again, maybe it was my preference for new challenges that was making me uncomfortable.

After a year of internal struggle, I decided to be "sort of" open to these requests to candidate. I decided that I would turn down any offer the first time, but I promised God that if any of those churches contacted me again, I would seriously consider the opportunity. Of course, I was not obligated to accept a call from any church where I might candidate.

During that year when I was struggling with my openness to move, I searched my heart and began to understand one reason why I'd made a lifetime commitment to the church in Virginia. I had wanted to avoid having to make another major decision.

Finally, after seven years of ministry, I announced to my Virginia church my resignation from ministry to them and acceptance of a call from another church which had contacted me the "required" second time. God gave me wisdom and direction for this very difficult decision. We were leaving people whom we loved and to whom we had committed ourselves for a "lifetime" which had lasted only seven years. Yet I honestly believe that had it not been for that initial "lifetime" commitment, I would not have stayed as long as I did.

Leaving Virginia raised other questions in my mind. What did I now believe about longevity? Is "lifetime" a realistic commitment for any pastor to make to a church? Can we plan longevity? Are the pressures of "ladder-climbing" in the pastorate too great to resist? What about me? What kind of pastor and person am I to have committed myself for a lifetime and then to leave after seven years? I wondered what the Virginia church people thought of me. Some were deeply hurt. Others asked me about my lifetime commitment. I wasn't even sure what I thought about myself. And more importantly, I wasn't sure what God thought of me.

These questions followed me to my new church. The pain of pastoral transitions, which church consultant Roy Oswald refers to in his booklets *The Pastor as Newcomer* and *Running through the Thistles*, became real to me. More than ever, I needed to reach some new conclusions about longevity. I needed a realistic view of how long a pastor could and should stay in one church. My idealism of a lifetime commitment and my once-in-a-lifetime chance to make and keep that commitment were gone. That left me searching for answers.

Since that first move to Wisconsin, where I also served a shorter pastorate than I had planned—just over three years—I have moved on to yet another place of ministry in Florida. As I write now, I am in my seventh year of ministry in Florida, beginning to enjoy some of the stability that comes with longevity.

The chance to study and write about pastoral longevity was provided in a post-graduate program of study at Bethel Seminary, St. Paul, Minnesota. My research is the basis for this book. My thoughts, however, are much more than the thoughts of a distant researcher. They are the heart musings of a pastor who has moved on. I write as someone who, in his own evaluation, "tried and failed" at longevity.

I BELIEVE . . .

I still believe in pastoral longevity even though my idealism as a young seminarian has been eroded by the hard realities of ministry, even after learning how difficult it is to commit oneself to a church, and even after recognizing that my natural bent is toward frequent change.

I do not think, however, that pastoral longevity is the only issue a pastor and a church should think about. Nor is it the *summum bonum* of ministry, as Jacob Eppinga, pastor since 1954 at LaGrave Avenue Christian Reformed Church in Grand Rapids, Michigan, can attest.

When asked about relocating, Eppinga responded, "I am not saying it is wrong to move. I believe the Lord has all kinds of ministers—some starters, some relievers, some sprinters, some milers. So the right length for one is not necessarily the right length for another. But all of us have to meet the challenge where we are, instead of leaving it unresolved."[10]

William Hobgood, author of an unpublished thesis entitled "Long-Tenured Pastorate," concurs. "The jury is not yet in on how long a pastorate should be to be successful, nor will it ever be! For there is no magic tenure. Every pastor-parish relationship is unique."[11]

Yet while pastoral longevity may not be the most important issue for a pastor and people to understand, I believe it is one which for too long has been ignored. While there may be a few men whose specific role in ministry is short-term pastorates for specific purposes, I believe the studies, interviews and data presented here indicate that there are many more short-term pastors than there are ministries requiring short-term pastors. Robert Schuller was right when he said, "The typical pastor comes to the church without the determination to stay there long enough to make it a great church."[12]

A study of long-term pastorates by the Alban Institute of Washington, D.C., reported on a "discovery of powerful evidence favoring long pastorates" and concluded that "in many ways, maintaining a healthy long pastorate is more difficult than changing pastorates every five years."[13] The study also noted a beginning trend toward long-term pastorates. It is my hope that this book will encourage that trend.

THE MASCULINE PASTOR

Throughout the book, I refer to the pastor with the masculine pronoun "he." I have done this for two reasons.

First, all the statistics, interviews and research upon which this book is based reflect only the situations of male senior pastors. Consequently, the discussions and conclusions in this paper more directly apply to men than to women in ministry. This does not mean, however, that most of the principles dealing with pastoral longevity are not just as applicable to women in positions of senior pastor.

Second, the majority of senior pastors, denominational leaders and lay people who read this book are presently under the ministry of a male senior pastor. My discussion of the concerns of pastoral longevity will be applied by them to their current experience with a male senior pastor. The transference of information and understanding will be easier for the majority of them if the pastor is referred to with the masculine pronoun.

However, as I have reflected on the need for longevity and stability in the North American church, I have started wondering what the longevity patterns would be were the majority of our pastors women. For instance, is it the male drive to measure success quantitatively that fuels the frequent desire to change pastorates? Would the female pastor's generally greater sense of nurturing encourage longer ministries? Of all the assumptions we make about pastors and the training we give them, how much is more a commentary on masculine values rather than a reflection of Christ-like ministry?

In any case, I trust that those who minister in other contexts will be able to expand the applications and conclusions of this book to include pastors in other settings and other traditions.

CAN A LEOPARD CHANGE HIS SPOTS?

Did you hear the one about the church schoolteacher who asked the class if a leopard could change his spots? They all shook their heads, "no," except one little girl who nodded, "yes." The teacher asked again if a leopard could change his spots, and again they all shook they heads except for the one little girl, who again nodded.

The teacher asked her what she meant by that, and the child answered, "I don't know why a leopard who doesn't like his spot can't go to another one."

This book is about pastors who "change their spots." While it is not my intent to suggest that a pastor can't change his spot if he doesn't like his spot, it is my hope that he will change his spots less frequently.

Endnotes

1. Eugene Peterson, "The Jonah Syndrome," *Leadership*, Summer 1990, pp. 41–43.
2. Lyle Schaller, "Whatever Happened to the Baby Boomers?" *MPL Journal*, Vol. VI, No. 1 (1985).
3. Stephen Sorenson, "Moving Targets: Ministry in a Transient Society," *Leadership*, Fall 1991, p. 123.
4. Lyle Schaller, *Hey, That's Our Church* (Nashville, TN: Abingdon, 1975), p. 96.
5. Kevin Miller, *Secrets of Staying Power* (Waco, TX: Word, 1988), p. 136.
6. Bill Ligon, *Discipleship: The Jesus View* (Plainfield, NJ: Logos, 1979), p. 218.
7. C. Peter Wagner, *Your Spiritual Gifts Can Help Your Church Grow* (Ventura, CA: Regal, 1979), p. 163.
8. Gary McIntosh, "Is It Time to Leave?" *Leadership*, Summer 1986, p. 71.
9. Darius Salter, *What Really Matters in Ministry* (Grand Rapids, MI:

Baker, 1990), pp. 32–33.

10. "Shepherds Who Have Stayed," *Leadership*, Fall 1983, p. 138.

11. William Hobgood, "The Long-Tenured Pastorate: A Study of Ways to Build Trust," Unpublished Thesis, Lancaster (PA) Seminary, 1982, p. 87.

12. Robert Schuller, *Your Church Has Real Possibilities* (Glendale, CA: Regal, 1974), p. 73.

13. Roy Oswald et al., *New Visions for the Long Pastorate* (Washington, DC: Alban Institute, 1983), p. 87.

• CHAPTER ONE •

THE NEED

I sat in a parsonage living room in northern Minnesota, listening to Bob (not his real name) share his story of a lifetime of short-term pastorates. He was near tears as he talked about church after church which he had served for no longer than three or four years and then moved on. Some of those moves were voluntary, others were made under pressure, and some were at the request or suggestion of a denominational leader. I felt awkward as I listened to him share his ministerial pain. I felt like I should be sitting behind some confessional curtain, out of sight.

Now in his early 60s, Bob was approaching retirement. And he knew it all too well. He pointed through the living room window to the small white chapel across the parsonage lawn. He guessed that this rural pastorate would be his last. It was a Norman Rockwellian setting: quaint, rustic and barren. The church was quaint and rustic; Bob was barren.

I almost felt as if he was complaining to me. Complaining about his lot in life to have served so many short-term pastorates. He hadn't planned his ministry career that way. It had just happened. I also felt as if he was pleading with me. Pleading to somehow change the unchangeable. To go back and start over. To restore to him all that he felt he had lost.

Bob lamented his lack of relational roots, his lack of retirement funds, and his lack of settledness. He felt sorry for his wife who had had to move so often, leaving friends behind time and time again. He felt sorry that he had moved again and again, hoping to climb the ecclesiastical ladder only to find out that the ladder he was climbing was suspended in midair. And he blamed a lifetime of short-term pastorates for all of it.

A FELT NEED

In interview after interview with denominational leaders, I have found that they, too, recognize pastoral longevity as an area that needs improving. In interview after interview with pastors and lay people, I have heard responses like these when I have asked about the need for pastors to stay longer:

> "The devil does not want to see long-term pastorates."
>
> "The national average is 1½ years. . . . There is a need to turn that around. [I am] hoping the pastor can stick around and become a part of the community."
>
> "Doesn't (our particular denomination) have a reputation for short-term pastors?"
>
> "There needs to be more long-term pastors in evangelical churches."
>
> "I didn't know any different than that pastors changed every four to five years."
>
> "It seems to be the (name of denomination) mindset for pastors to change every so often. There is a 'ripple effect' every couple of years as pastors change churches."

In another survey that asked clergy about the issue of pastoral longevity, Ross Scherer discovered that 30 percent of the clergy questioned felt that pastors were "moving around too much."[1]

While it is true that pastors remain in their *vocation* longer than workers in almost any other profession—an average of 15.8 years, longer than elementary school teachers, physicians or lawyers[2]—the problem seems to be that they do not stay long in one spot.

THE LONG AND SHORT OF IT

What does it mean to stay long? How long is "long"? How short is "short"? When I asked a sampling of clergy and laity the question, "How long do you think a pastor should stay in one church, on the average?" I got a variety of answers:

> "He can't be effective in less than five years"
> "Based upon my personal experience in the ministry, six to seven years."
> "A good average would be 12 to 15 years."
> "At least four to five years, then plan to stay at least two to three years after that."
> "No less than seven to eight years to touch the community."
> "No less than 12 to 15 years to touch the county."

Other opinions among clergy and laity alike put the minimum number of years they thought a pastor should stay at one church at between 3–10 years and the maximum at between 8–15 years.

When I went to studies and authors who attempted to address in whole or in part the issue of pastoral longevity, I got more of the same—differing but interesting opinions for differing and interesting reasons. For instance, in their study of long pastorates, associates with the Alban Institute of Washington,

D.C., cited a "widely current norm in many denominations for pastors to stay in a given church for at least five years, but no longer than 10 years."[3] By their definition, a "short" pastorate would be about five years, a "long" pastorate would last about 10 years. Elsewhere, the study talked about developing an intervention strategy in longer pastorates to insure a healthier ministry in the years ahead, should the pastor remain. The authors felt that such an intervention ought to occur somewhere between the eighth and 12th year of a pastor's ministry in a particular church. Their plan suggests that intervention ought to occur before "long-term gaps" (discussed in chapter three) appear. The inference seems to be that a "long" pastorate could be considered any ministry lasting from eight to 12 years.[4]

In a later conversation I had with Roy Oswald, one of the authors of the Alban Institute study, he stated that a pastor and his congregation needed to renegotiate his role after six to eight years. This advice suggests that, after six to eight years, adjustments for a longer pastorate should be made. The inference is that "long" means any time longer than eight years.

On the other hand, author William Hobgood defines a "long-tenured pastor" as one who stays 10 years. His choice of this length of time was based on two premises. First, he said that from his experience in the pastorate and from what he had learned from other pastors who have had significantly longer pastorates, he now believes that except for extremely large or extremely small congregations, it takes about eight years for the pastor to "catch up" with all of the various parishioners' personal and family crises. His opinion is that it requires about eight to 10 years for the pastor to develop strong personal ties across the whole congregation's life.

Hobgood's other reason for selecting 10 years as his definition of a long-tenured pastor is strongly influenced by the work of

Daniel Levinson. Levinson studied the adult male life cycles and found that in the course of a man's adult life, he will experience several "stable periods." During these stable periods, Levinson says, the primary task for the person is to "build a life structure . . . make certain key choices, form a structure around them, and pursue one's goals and values within that structure." The closing comment from Levinson seems to have been the key to Hobgood's definition of long-tenured. Levinson said that a stable period ordinarily lasts six or seven years, *10 at the most!* Ten years appeared to him to be the natural "life-cycle season" in a man's life.

Hobgood combined his own observation and study with Levinson's and concluded that "Further study would show, it appears likely, that most pastors who are in long pastorates began these near the beginning of one of the six-to-10-year cycles that Levinson identifies as natural in all adult males: that is to say, at about age 25, 30, 40, or 50." Then Hobgood takes a giant step beyond this initial application of Levinson's observations which had influenced him toward the 10-year definition of long-term. He tells us that Levinson's study helps us to see that for a pastor to stay, literally, in the "same place" for over 10 years "might go against the natural developmental grain of adult males."[5] Could the suggestion here be that not only is 10 years to be considered long-term, but maybe it also ought to be considered long enough?

When we talk about how long a pastorate should be, Gerard Gillaspie adds that "experience has proven that about five years are needed to do any lasting work." He says, "Ten years is the suggested average for other than the first pastorate, but beyond ten is questionable for the average man." Then he quotes an Edward Byington who says that only after the first pastorate might a man think about having a 10-year pastorate. Among the churches that Byington was familiar with, the pastorates that have continued much beyond 10 years have usually proved anti-climatic. He does admit, however, that there have been some noteworthy exceptions. His general impression is that while most pastors move too much, "the spirit and demands of this age are such that few men can impress, inspire and guide for much more than ten years the same body of people."[6] While I disagree with the idea that a 10-year pastorate is long enough, I do recognize the problems that can develop and the need to help pastors and churches to avoid hitting the 10-year wall. Something tells me there doesn't have to be a crash!

And the variations on the meaning of short and long continue. One author defined short pastorates as four years or less. Another study inferred that "short" equals anything less than four years and "very long" as anything 12 years or more. Yet Alban Institute's study of long-tenured pastors chose seven pastors averaging 17.4 years of ministry in their present church and in William Hobgood's independent study, the average length of stay for pastors he reviewed was 15.5 years.

In their survey of "Shepherds Who Have Stayed," *Leadership Journal* chose four pastors who averaged 32 years in their present pastorate! Lyle Schaller tells the story of a mythical Pastor Don Johnson, who is at a crossroads in his ministry after nine years. Schaller implies that this is a long time in one church, though it could become longer if Pastor Don so chose. Schaller is quoted elsewhere as saying that "the prime time for a pastor to consider moving is after eight years."[7]

After digesting all of these opinions and studies, I have reached the conclusion that "short" can be anything from four to seven years and "long" can be anything from eight to 32 years! For the sake of sane discussion and common ground, I have synthesized the data and research on what long and short mean into the following definitions. "Long" means any pastorate nine years or longer. "Short" means any pastorate lasting less than five years. Compared with all the other definitions, this understanding of these terms is as good as any and will be used as the basis for our discussion of short-term and long-term pastorates.

By now you should be tired of all this discussion of "short" and "long" (a long discussion or a short discussion, depending on your definition of short and long!). If so, you can thank our modern times. People didn't used to have to be so concerned over pastoral longevity.

THEN . . .

In American church history, the tendency toward short pastorates developed in reaction to early church life in New England where the minister was commonly settled for life.

The idea of life-long pastorates crossed the Atlantic with the early settlers. If you were to visit the cemetery of Bunhill Fields in London, you would notice the great number of pastors buried there who served their congregations for extended periods of time. Many of them served their particular church for more than 25 years, some of them serving a single congregation for as long as 50 years. One pastor, John Gill, who was in the pulpit later filled by Charles Spurgeon, served that church for more than 50 years. And the man who followed Gill served for 63 years! Spurgeon himself served in that same church for nearly 40 years.

So it came to be in early America that a pastor legally had life tenure, with dismissal possible only for unorthodox doctrine, neglect of duty, immorality or criminal conduct.

In an imaginary conversation, Lyle Schaller quotes a 235-year-old Congregational preacher:

I graduated from Yale in 1773. My class included sixteen men who entered the ministry in the Congregational Church. Ten served only one church in their whole life, and five others served only two pastorates. That was typical of the graduates of Yale in the eighteenth century. Very, very few served more than two congregations in their entire career. When you got a call, everyone assumed you would be with that congregation for the rest of your life. Now everybody expects a minister to move after a few years in one pastorate. It sure was easier back when a minister settled in and stayed in one place for the rest of his life! Close to half of the Congregational ministers of the eighteenth century served at least thirty years in one pastorate.[8]

While longevity was the rule in early America, there were always exceptions to the rule. Some things change in church ministry, but other things don't. Jonathan Edwards was dismissed from a short pastorate at the whim of a congregational majority!

By the 19th century, the American people began to assume that a pastor's zeal declined after the first three years, and by the fourth year, a pastoral change was expected. In fact, one denomination established a four-year tenure for pastors, hoping to keep church and pastor from growing static. And when several other denominations followed their example, the practice of frequently changing pastors became standard policy.[9]

This tradition of a four-year pastorate developed from the ministry of Francis Asbury and the early circuit riders who spent six weeks to six months building a church and then moved on. The pastoral stay of these traveling preachers gradually stretched to one year, then two. By the early 20th century, four-year appointments were common. Such four-year pastorates are still enforced by some denominations. As one writer put it, this "connectional itinerant system" really meant, "keep your bags packed and never unpack your books."[10]

Over time, preachers began actually to favor shorter pastorates. They seemed to find it easier to change congregations than to prepare new sermons! Besides, the newness and glamour of a pastorate faded after two or three years, and the pastor began looking for greener fields. One study done of the ministerial empire of William Bell Riley (former president of Northwestern Bible College) in the 1930s and 40s revealed that the average length of pastorates for his college's ministry graduates was 3.76 years. It seems that many of these alumni were afflicted with a yen for upward mobility to those greener fields.[11]

Used by permission of Dan Schmidt.

. . . AND NOW

Today, short-term pastorates appear to be the norm. In reports from denominations around the country, the picture is much the same. The American Lutheran Church anticipates a 20 percent turnover of its clergy annually. They reported that their pastors moved on the average once every four years.[12]

The Disciples of Christ denomination cites the average tenure of its pastors as being four years. In the Evangelical Free Church of America, it is 4.74 years; in the Baptist General Conference, it is 4.56 years; and in the Lutheran Church/Missouri Synod, the average length of stay for a pastor is between 3.3 years and 3.6 years.[13] Statistics from my own denomination (The Christian and Missionary Alliance) reveal an average tenure of 4.5 years.

Others have come up with similar numbers:

"The average pastor lasts twenty-eight months in our denomination."[14]

"The Southern Baptist pastor moves on the average every 18–24 months"[15]

"In our denomination, the average stay of a rural pastor is 33 months. That means a child growing up in a rural church will have had seven pastors by age 18.[16]

Wherever you look the story is the same. In denomination after denomination, there is little variation from the national norm of four years for the length of time a pastor stays where he is. Somehow, the vow of stability has gotten lost in the frantic search for whatever it is pastors and churches are looking for.

A CLOSER LOOK

A few years ago, I wanted to take a little closer look at some of these statistics on pastoral longevity. So I took a sampling of over 100 churches and pastors that was representative of the national figures on pastoral longevity. Here is what I discovered, based on a study of longevity statistics since 1920.

In this representative sampling, only 35 percent of the pastorates lasted longer than five years. I was shocked to discover that less than five percent of the pastorates lasted longer than 10 years. I was saddened to find out that almost one in five churches had *never* had a pastor more than five years and almost three-quarters of the churches had *never* had a pastor more than 10 years!

I also learned that the average length of a pastor's stay was at its lowest in the 1920s (2.3–2.6 years) and highest in the 1960s (5.2–5.4 years). The greatest decade for pastoral transfers was the 1970s. It was particularly interesting to note that city churches fared only slightly better in keeping their pastors longer. The average length of ministry in "rural" churches ("rural" defined as communities with less than 50,000 population) was 4.3 years. The average length of ministry in "urban" churches (churches in communities with a population greater than 50,000) was 4.9 years. When I compared rural and urban longevity patterns, I found that 61 percent of urban churches and 77 percent of rural churches had never had a pastor stay longer than 10 years.

Researcher Ronald Wimberly discovered the same patterns in his review of longevity statistics in rural and city churches. He also found that the size of the church was less important than the location—a pastor was more likely to stay longer in a smaller urban church than a larger rural church.[17] But the difference is minor; regardless of church size or location, the lack of pastoral longevity is pervasive.

All of the information I gathered and studied only confirmed what I had felt for years—a majority of pastors and churches had never experienced a long-term pastorate. Pastors weren't staying longer where they were. The system was breeding instability in pastors and in churches.

THE PROFESSIONAL AND THE HIPPIE

This pattern of short-term pastorates seems to be kept alive in our day by two clergy models which James Glasse describes as the "professional" model and the "ecclesiastical hippie" model.

Glasse uses the image of a "magical machine" to illustrate the professional model of ministry. Let's say that a pastor has been in a particular parish for a number of years. One day he is sitting in his study, musing to himself. "I have been pastor of this church for five years. I have had a useful ministry here. But I think I have done about all I can in this place. Perhaps it is time for me to move on."

Put that into Glasse's "machine," push the "professional" button and here is what comes out . . . Lawyer: "I've been practicing law in this town for five years. I have had a good practice, and done very well. But I think I have done about all I can in this place. Perhaps I should move on." Glasse then asks the question, "What sense does that make?"

Or put the same pastoral comment into the machine again and push the professional button a second time then listen. Teacher: "I have been teaching third grade for 10 years. I have taught a lot of children. But I think I have done about all I can in this school. Perhaps it is time for me to move on." Once again Glasse asks, "What sense does it make for a teacher to talk like this?"

One more time put the pastor's comment into the machine and push the same professional button again and listen. Doctor: "I have been a doctor in this town for seven years. I have helped a lot of people and improved the services of the hospital. But I think I have done about all I can do in this place. Perhaps it is time to move on."[18]

How does what our pastor says to himself in his own study sound when it comes from the lips of other professionals in his town? A little peculiar, don't you think? So what makes this the "professional" thing for a pastor to say? Yet the "professional" model for clergy now includes this kind of personal dialogue.

The "ecclesiastical hippie" model describes the pastor who goes around doing his own thing. And when his thing doesn't work any more, he goes somewhere else and does his thing all over again. And when he gets bored he goes somewhere else and does his thing there.

This "hippie" pastor, 15 years in the business of pastoring, has moved three times. He hasn't had 15 years of ministry experience; he's had five years experience three different times! He never has to change anything but his location. He never learns. He never grows. He doesn't have to. The system is designed to maximize his idiosyncracies and make it possible for him to keep alive the illusion of his creativity simply by moving around.[19]

It is with the use of such self-talk and self-delusion that the pattern of short-term pastorates is supported. This kind of thinking and this kind of career path will have to change if pastors and churches are to ever experience the benefits of longer pastorates. Just maybe, some of that change is on the horizon.

NEW TRENDS?

Could we hope for a change in these patterns? Maybe. Maybe not. Figures and trends from the last 25 years give the impression of a slight increase in pastoral longevity in some areas of the country among certain church groups. For example, as recently as 1969, the Massachusetts Diocese of the Episcopal Church reported 25 percent of their pastorates as being long-term (by our definition). Ten years later, in 1979, that figure was up to 39 percent. Could this selective sampling indicate that perhaps there is a growing awareness and desire for more stability among some pastors and churches?

Before we get too excited and prematurely declare a new trend of longer pastorates nationwide, these figures from the north-eastern United States of more than a decade ago must be countered with statistics recently released by Kirk Hadaway (author of a new book *Church Growth Principles*). He noted that the average pastoral tenure among Protestant denominations in the U.S. today was still only 3.7 years.[20] There is still much work to be done.

However, there are several factors at work today that have the potential of influencing pastors and churches to work together for longer pastorates:

1) Relocation expense—the increasing cost of moving makes staying more attractive for both pastor and church.

2) Clergy surplus—in some mainline denominations, there are more clergy than pastorates. The leaders in some churches have announced in recent years that they will limit the number of ministerial appointments and give preference to pastors over 40 years of age. In some of these denominations, the clergy-parish picture is of a "buyer's market," in which congregations tend to have more control over a minister's career than he does, thus pressing some clergy to work harder at staying than they might have otherwise.

3) Clergy shortage—while the mainline denominations may experience a clergy surplus, the same cannot be said for some of the more conservative church groups. In his recent book,

Leith Anderson predicts a coming shortage of clergy. "There will be a switch from the recent buyer's market to a seller's market. Churches will have a much more difficult time finding pastors." As many as 30 to 40 percent of pastors currently serving American churches will reach retirement age by the year 2000. If a clergy surplus causes pastors to think twice about moving and risking the possibility of not finding a church available, a clergy shortage may cause churches to think twice about changing pastors so often. Anderson comments that churches "will work much harder to retain those [pastors] they have."[21]

4) Spouse careers—clergy spouses are working in increasing numbers, for both economic and vocational reasons. The pastor contemplating a move may have two careers to consider.

5) Home ownership—more clergy are choosing to buy their own homes rather than living in church-owned parsonages. Home ownership makes a pastor think twice before leaving too soon.

6) Sabbaticals—sabbatical leaves provide a temporary break from the pastorate, giving the pastor time to renew himself through continuing education, rather than a move.

7) Salary parity—a leveling of salaries among pastors in the same denomination results in a smaller difference between the salaries of larger and smaller churches and gives a pastor less reason to make moves that would advance him up the economic ladder.

8) Parishioner mobility—since the laity seems to be in transition themselves (one out of every five Americans relocates every year), a pastor can stay at the same church but minister to a different congregation without moving.

These factors and more may eventually encourage pastors to stay longer in pastorates. But let me hasten to add that there are greater reasons for increasing longevity. Reasons not related to salary, shortages or surpluses, but reasons connected to the meaning of ministry itself. We will talk about some of those deeper issues later.

In our desire to see pastorates last longer, we must realize, however, that not all of these longer stays will be healthy ones. As Roy Oswald has observed, "I suspect that there are situations where the pastor is holding on for dear life, and the congregation is doing the same, staying together where, in years before, a more mobile clergy might have moved."[22]

Yet far too often the reverse is true. The pastor lets go too soon. Lyle Schaller writes,

> From the congregation's perspective the most effective years of a pastorate rarely begin before the fourth or fifth or sixth or seventh, and sometimes even the eighth, year of that pastorate. What does this pattern say to the question, "Has the time come for me to move?" In a majority of pastorates it probably means that if that question is being asked before the fourth or fifth year of that pastorate, it is premature. If that question is being asked in the third year, the response may be, "Don't move, your best years here have yet to begin." If asked in the fifth or sixth year, the appropriate response may be, "Why think about moving when you are just beginning your best years in this pastorate?"[23]

Whatever the reasons for any increase in the length of a pastor's stay, and there are some good reasons as well as bad ones, pastors need to find within themselves and the system needs to provide them with support for improving the record of pastoral longevity. For too long it seems like the average American pastor has moved right along with all the other relocating Americans. For too long pastors have moved without asking the right questions. For too long American congregations have watched their pastors move around and not known what to do about it.

WHAT ABOUT BOB?

I had no easy answers for Bob. I couldn't undo what had already been done. The best I could do was listen to his anguish. As a younger pastor, with years ahead of me to avoid his pain, I sat feeling a little guilty that I had the chance to sidestep what he could not. When he finished, he thanked me for listening, we prayed together, and then I left.

As I drove away, I knew that this was not an isolated case. There were other "Bobs" out there who were experiencing the same thing. Without planning for it, without thinking about it, they, their churches, their denominations and the ecclesiastical "system" would sentence them to a ministry life of short-term pastorates without ever giving them the chance for pastoral longevity.

I knew that something had to be done. I knew that we had to start asking questions that would raise both an awareness of and hunger for longer pastorates among pastors, churches and denominational leaders. Something inside me said that for the most part, longer was better. Now more than ever, all of us must start thinking about restoring that old vow of stability.

Endnotes

1. Allen Nauss and Harry Coiner, "The First Parish: Stayers and Movers," *Review of Religious Research,* Winter 1971, p. 96.

2. *U.S. News and World Report*, January 23, 1989, p. 66.

3. Roy Oswald et al., *New Visions for the Long Pastorate* (Washington, DC: Alban Institute, 1983), p. 27.

4. Ibid. p. 18.

5. William Hobgood, "The Long-Tenured Pastorate: A Study of Ways to Build Trust," Unpublished Thesis, Lancaster (PA) Seminary, 1982, pp. 2–4.

6. Gerard Gillaspie, *The Restless Pastor* (Chicago: Moody, 1974), pp. 17, 22.

7. Lyle Schaller, *Survival Tactics in the Parish*, (Nashville: Abingdon, 1977), pp. 22–24.

8. Lyle Schaller, *It's a Different World* (Nashville: Abingdon, 1988), p. 10.

9. Gillaspie, *The Restless Pastor*, p. 13.

10. Ibid.

11. William Trollinger, Jr., "Riley's Empire," *The Best in Theology III* (Carol Stream, IL: CT Inc., 1989), p. 118.

12. Roy Oswald, *The Pastor as Newcomer* (Washington, DC: Alban Institute, 1977), p. 1.

13. These statistics are quoted from the following sources: Disciples of Christ—William Hobgood, "The Long-Tenured Pastorate: A Study of Ways to Build Trust," p. 86. Evangelical Free Church and the Baptist General Conference—Gerald Gillaspie, *The Restless Pastor*, p. 15. Lutheran Church, Missouri Synod—Allen Nauss, "The Relation of Pastoral Mobility to Effectiveness," *Review of Religious Research*, Winter 1974, p. 82.

14. Calvin Miller, "Fiddlin' with the Staff," *Leadership*, Winter 1986, p. 104.

15. Frank Tillapaugh, *Unleashing the Church* (Ventura, CA: Regal, 1982), p. 12.

16. Stephen McMullin, "In the Pastoral Pastorate," *Leadership*, Summer 1987, p. 73.

17. Ronald Wimberly, "Mobility in Ministerial Career Patterns: Exploration," *Journal of the Scientific Study of Religion*, Vol. 10, 1971, pp. 249–253.

18. James Glasse, *Putting It Together in the Parish* (Nashville: Abingdon, 1972), pp. 23–24.

19. Ibid. pp. 45–46.

20. *The Win Arn Report*, Number 36, 1992.

21. Leith Anderson, *A Church for the 21st Century* (Minneapolis: Bethany, 1992), p. 79.

22. Oswald et al., *New Visions*, pp. 87–88.

23. Schaller, *Survival Tactics*, p. 27.

• CHAPTER TWO •

THE SHORT STORY

For decades the small midwestern church watched young college and seminary graduates come to be their pastor. The church people looked on as these pastors stayed long enough to get ministry experience that would look good on their resumes. Most of them lasted only a year or two, usually leaving for a less rural, slightly larger church.

The only break in this pattern was when a missionary candidate came to fill the pulpit. The candidate's mandatory "home service" requirement guaranteed the church the same pastor for at least two years—which was longer than some of their other pastors had stayed. But even these "missionaries-in-training" only confirmed the church in its opinion of itself: they were just the first stop for young men on their way to somewhere else.

As I listened to the church's lay leaders talk about their history, I got the impression that initially the church resisted and resented this pattern of revolving-door pastors. But as their story continued, it seemed the church went through a period of time when they resigned themselves to it. Short-term pastorates weren't exactly what they wanted, but if that is what it took to have a pastor, they could live with it.

By the time these church people got around to telling me about the church's more recent past, I heard a new attitude that shocked me. Instead of resenting being treated like a doormat, instead of resigning themselves to having pastor after pastor stay less than two years, this church had started—if you can believe this—to take some pride in their pattern of short-term pastors. They had actually come to view themselves as playing a unique role in their denomination. They were the church where the young bucks got broken in! Short-term pastorates had given this church what little identity it had.

NOT SO BAD AFTER ALL?

Could it be that short-term pastorates aren't so bad after all? Maybe long-term pastorates aren't the "greater good" of church ministry their supporters claim. After all, not everyone thinks that longer is better or shorter is worse. As one pastor said, "I just can't say that long-term is for everybody." Roy Oswald, Director of Field Studies and Training at the Alban Institute, Washington, D.C., once told me, "Some men make good short-term pastors. They like conflict and adventure!"

Short-term pastorates and long-term pastorates both have their adventures and misadventures, their advantages and disadvantages. An honest look at each one is bound to raise our awareness of the issues surrounding pastoral longevity. And whether you are a pastor or a layperson, it will help you to understand what it means for a church and its pastor to consider taking the vow of stability.

SOMETHING GOOD MIGHT HAPPEN

The truth is, good things can happen in short-term pastorates. One layperson reported that his church grew more in one two-year pastorate than in the seven-year pastorate that followed. Another saw the brighter side of having a two-year missionary candidate for a pastor: "It increased our missionary vision."

You already know my choice is for pastors staying longer, so I won't try to fool you. While I will discuss the advantages of short-term pastorates, I will also raise some questions, and later in this book I will elaborate on these questions. With that in mind, let's take a look at some of the most common advantages of a short-term pastorate:

1. *A specific task can be accomplished.* Sometimes a short-term pastor can accomplish something which might be too difficult or unpopular for a pastor planning to stay longer. Things like church "housecleaning," conflict resolution, transition after a long pastorate, completion of a building program or church reorganization may be more easily attempted when both the church and the pastor know that they won't have to live with each other after the trench work is over.

There is no denying the need for pastoral "problem-solvers," especially in the area of church revitalization. Harry Reader of Christ Covenant Church in Matthews, North Carolina has classified pastoral ministries into three categories: the organizing pastor (church planter), the continuing pastor (leading an established church in healthy growth), and the revitalizing pastor (for a once-flourishing church now on the decline). He believes that most pastors will be involved in revitalization at some time during their careers, since the number of healthy, growing churches is relatively small and their pulpits are available less frequently—the pastors of healthy, growing churches don't want to move.[1]

Church planting is another task that is sometimes better accomplished by a man whose stay is shorter rather than longer. This is usually because a man whose ministry gift is distinctly church planting will more than likely stay just long enough to get the church started (perhaps one or two years) and then move on to begin another work.

Seminary President David McKenna says that instead of condemning this kind of short-term pastor who is gifted in church planting, we should honor him for using his gifts in church ministry and moving on to start new churches. He writes that, "According to the viewpoint of waste and pollution, that minister should adapt to all of the seasons of church change and growth; but according to the recycling viewpoint of leadership resources, the same pastor would move to a new opportunity with dignity."[2]

There are times in a church's life and in the gift-mix of a pastor when a shorter pastorate is called for. When special and frequently unpopular tasks need to be accomplished for the health of a church, sometimes a shorter pastorate is better. But those times are much fewer and farther between than most people think.

2. *A church can receive a fresh start.* There are times when, after a difficult or disappointing pastorate, a new minister can bring vision, renewed zeal and a fresh outlook. Lyle Schaller makes the observation from his years of church consulting that if a congregation has plateaued or is declining, and the current pastor has been there for five years or longer, the church will probably not begin to grow again until the arrival of the next pastor.[3]

The conclusion that some would rush to, given this bit of information, is that a church with a frequent turnover in pastors would also experience constant rejuvenation. In fact, the opposite is true. A church like that is not energized, it is enervated.

3. *A pastor can experience new challenges.* If ministerial turnover can be a shot in the arm for a church, it can certainly

be true for a pastor as well. The short-term pastor is sure to feel rejuvenated with each fresh beginning at a new church. In fact, with each change in churches comes a fresh chance for the pastor to learn something more and experiment with new ideas and methods.

Jacob Eppinga, a pastor in Grand Rapids, Michigan talked about a two-year pastorate in his early days of ministry. "I left because I felt we were not quite right for each other. Maybe I was wrong to leave . . . but I thought they would be better served by a different type of minister. The short pastorate was right for me in that situation, I believe."[4]

With a change of scenery comes a chance to start over, a sense of new beginning, new friends, new incentives and even new energy. All that can't be bad, can it? While there is no question that a new beginning can bring with it a sense of renewing, a series of "renewals" is not the same as an opportunity for the personal development that takes place in staying longer. Actually, a man who is continually changing churches may not be renewed at all; he may be at best stunting his growth and at worst postponing a breakdown of some kind.

4. *A church's ministry can be improved.* Every pastor relates to a different set of people, in the church and in the community. Over the years, as pastors come and go, different people find points of identification with each new pastor. The result, as church folk wisdom has it, is that each new pastor adds to an ever-widening circle of influence for the church and its ministries.

In addition, you would think that a church which goes through the pastoral selection process every couple of years or so would get better at selecting a pastor. And doing a better job of picking the pastor would improve the quality and effectiveness of the church.

Also, some believe that churches with a long-term pastor tend to "go flat on one side." They contend that each new pastor brings a different set of gifts to the church, and laypeople will develop their gifts to complement the pastor's. This theory holds that a frequent turnover in pastors with differing gifts will, over the years, develop more laypeople in more areas of ministry, thus producing a well-rounded and active lay ministry.

These arguments may sound convincing, but they have little basis in fact. While long-term pastorates have their dangers (as we will see in the next chapter), the usual effects on a church with a pattern of short-term pastors are less effectiveness in the community and less lay involvement.

5. *Transitions for the pastor can be easier.* One of the most common benefits of short-term pastorates cited by laypeople is that it is easier for a pastor to move on because he hasn't become too deeply tied to the church or the community. Long-term pastorates cause the man and the church more pain when it's over, they say.

It is true that the longer a pastor stays the deeper his roots; this is also the very environment that is most conducive to significant ministry. Perhaps there is a bit of a trade-off here. Which do you want, easier transitions for pastors or deeper ministry for churches?

These first five advantages are the most frequent ones that have been suggested by pastors and laypeople. But these last two are ones you are not so apt to hear voiced, though I have found them to be in the back of many people's minds and maybe even on the tip of their tongues!

6. *There can be some relief for the church budget.* One of the advantages of changing pastors frequently is that a financially struggling church can use the time between pastors—when there is no pastor's salary to pay—to get caught up on the bills!

7. *There can be more church fellowships!* A church usually has more fellowships, get-togethers and pot-luck dinners during the candidating process than at any other time. Lyle Schaller has said that a series of short pastorates can result in a church developing a high level of competence in three areas: giving parties to welcome the new minister; providing social opportunities for the new minister to get acquainted with the people; and giving parties to bid farewell to the departing minister.[5] Once the new pastor is installed, the church returns to a more regular routine.

What can I say? These last two points are perhaps the least significant but the most honest admission of the advantages of short term pastorates that I have listed!

THE SHORT AND WINDING ROAD

As you read over this list of the advantages of short-term pastorates, did you get the feeling that someone is trying to make the best out of a bad situation? I have found that more and more pastors and laypeople are willing to admit that short-term ministry is not all it is cracked up to be.

For instance, when I asked pastors, "What effects on pastors of short-term pastorates have you experienced or observed?" this is what some of them said:

"Every move is harder. And it is harder on the pastor than it is on the church."

"It has been frustrating. I have the feeling that my task at that church was never finished."

"I don't want to live this kind of life over again" (shared by a pastor whose career had been a series of one short-term pastorate after another).

Did you hear some of their problems and pain?

And when I asked laypeople the question, "What effects on churches of short-term pastorates have you observed or experienced?" here is what some of them said (once again, listen to the feelings behind their answers):

> "It is hard on the church. It can be a strain on the church to have pastors moving in and out."
>
> "It makes the church feel insecure."
>
> "It becomes real easy to give up on the church."

The honesty of these pastors and laypeople is helping us

"In six years we've had six pastors who were really on fire. We'd like someone lukewarm for a while."

uncover the real truth about short-term pastorates. The short-term road can be painful, winding through hurts and problems that are all too often not discovered by pastors or churches soon enough. If you listen to some of those hurts and problems, you would come up with a list of the disadvantages of shorter pastorates that might look something like this:

1. *The church must adjust to constantly changing leadership.* A new pastor often proposes major program changes; a frequent change of pastors breeds resistance in laypeople to another new pastor coming in with yet another "bag of programs." And just when a pastor has been long enough at a church to get a lay leadership team in place to run his programs, he leaves. In many small churches, the pastor does not become an influential policy-maker before the third or fourth year of his tenure, just about the time he is getting ready to leave.

This constant change in leadership and leadership styles hurts the church, causing depression, friction and confusion in the people. One layperson said to me, "It takes up to two years for a church to heal from the trauma of a pastor leaving." Whether his comment is factual or not, the truth is that as a layperson, his involvement in his local church will be affected by how he evaluates the frequent turnover of pastors. I know of one church that closed because short-term pastorates caused so much leadership instability that the church broke apart.

There is overwhelmingly persuasive evidence that the most productive years of a pastorate seldom begin before the fourth to sixth year of a minister's tenure. By changing pastors frequently, a congregation has an excellent chance of missing out on some very productive years of ministry.

2. *The church's ministry to the community suffers.* If the church barely has time to adjust to a new person at the top, the community has even less of an opportunity. The trust that a

community might have in a pastor or church is greatly hindered by a series of short-term pastorates. Ministry that the church could and should have among area leaders, business persons and school officials disappears when the community gets the impression that a church's pastors won't be there very long and will soon "flit" to another church.

3. *The continuity of ministry is affected.* In answer to those who think that "fresh starts" is one of the advantages of short-term pastorates, one lay leader with whom I talked saw no silver lining in new beginnings or a constant change in programs and leadership. He very clearly expressed his frustration at "having to start over with each new pastor."

Many times a pastor builds a church and then leaves when he is most needed to help maintain the momentum. With a frequent turnover of pastors, a church can very easily lose its sense of direction and identity, spending more time going sideways, adjusting to new pastors, than going forward, advancing in ministry.

New pastors often begin their pulpit ministries with similar themes, usually a series on basic Christian beliefs or the nature of the church. This means that a church will get those same basics reviewed again and again when they more than likely need, like the readers of the book of Hebrews (6:1–2), to move on to deeper truths of the Christian life and ministry. One lay person I spoke with said that it takes two or three times as long for a believer to be discipled and become mature when the church has experienced multiple pastors in a brief span of time than it does with one pastor who stays longer.

4. *There is a lack of church growth.* It is a well-known fact that every time a pastor leaves, some church people leave too. Either they were loyal only to the man and not the church, or they were using the pastor's departure as a convenient time to

do what they were going to do anyway, change churches. Schaller observes, "A growing body of evidence suggests that the largest single factor in explaining why people drop out of church or leave for another congregation without changing their place of residence is a change in pastors."[6]

In addition, as was mentioned above, a frequent turnover in pastors makes effective outreach into the community harder and harder. This lack of outreach affects church growth. Some of this lack of growth comes from the limitations a short-term pastorate sets on goal setting. If a pastor sees himself as being at his present church five years or less, his goals tend to be stunted, either by his short-sighted vision or by the lack of trust from the people that only comes when a pastor has stayed long enough to build that trust.

Not only is there a lack of numerical growth, but personal and spiritual growth as well. When C. Philip Hinerman, pastor since 1952 at Park Avenue United Methodist Church in Minneapolis, Minnesota, was asked about the weaknesses of short-term pastorates, he answered, "You never solve the problems. The chance to grow, to work through hostilities, to reconcile is forfeited. . . . Over time, a small coterie, a power clique, begins to rule that congregation, killing the preacher whenever the preacher doesn't suit their fancy. It's so sad."[7]

Through a series of short-term pastorates, a church develops immature patterns of dealing with problems. Acting more like George Steinbrenner than the Church of Jesus Christ, they think it is easier to fire the coach than fire up the players. Like a spoiled child that gets its way, a church stunts its spiritual growth through the "quick-fix" method of dealing with problems by keeping pastorates short.

5. *The self-image of the church suffers.* Of all the effects on churches of short-term pastorates, this one cuts the deepest. I

will never forget the pain in the voice of the layperson from a church that had experienced several consecutive short-term pastorates when she said "You feel embarrassed. . . . You don't want to invite people to your church. . . . You are apprehensive about new Christians coming to your church." Those who attend a church with a history of short-term pastorates do not feel good about themselves or their church. It is difficult for most laypeople to be consistently enthusiastic about their church and their pastor if there is a change in ministers every two or three years.

And when people don't feel good about their church, it also affects their sense of community with each other. One layperson made this observation about how short-term pastorates had affected his church: "We can't seem to develop that family feeling in the church."

At times, short-term pastorates cause painful introspection by the church and its leaders. As one lay leader put it, "I would like to know what we are doing wrong that does not allow us to keep a man for a longer time." Another said to me, "In 13 years, this church has had five pastors. . . . We begin to think, 'what is wrong with us?' " Just how deep this introspection can go is reflected in this layperson's comment to me: "I used to feel guilty that all these pastors left."

This pain from short pastorates that laity feel but don't often talk about is perhaps most poignantly expressed by the layperson who shared, "I look upon pastors' leaving like a divorce—grief, hurt, guilt and more. I ask myself, 'What could I have done differently? Where did I fail?' There is trauma each time."

6. *The pastor and his family suffer.* First, there is the financial loss. Many pastors lose money each time they move. They experience few of the perks and little of the security of a longer pastorate. They usually don't get the chance to buy their own

home or establish a good financial foundation.

Then there is the emotional loss. The frequent change in pastorates can make a pastor's family feel insecure. One pastor I talked to, who was himself a preacher's kid, said to me, "I got tired of moving around." Another said it took his children three years to feel completely settled after each move. Another reflected, "It is hard on the kids, always moving."

Beneath the advertised "adventure" in moving to a new city and meeting new friends, is the pain of starting over again and again. One pastor shared, "It takes about two years for a pastor's wife to settle into a new area and a new church—emotionally and socially." And just about that time, it seems, her husband is beginning to think about moving. Research shows that a substantial number of pastors are very receptive to the idea of moving to another congregation only 35–45 months after arriving in their current pastorate.[8] One pastor wrote, "Few will mourn the resignation of a pastor after that brief a stay (three years or so). It's expected. But for the pastor, breaking up is damaging to the ego, to the family, and the pocketbook. Changing churches is stressful, and I've hardly moved out of love for packing tape."[9]

7. *There is a lack of depth in personal relationships.* With short-term ministries, the pastor and the people have little chance to get to know each other. One short-term pastor admitted, "I have found it difficult to develop deep, close friends, and so has my family."

And getting to know and trust each other is a must for ministry to take place. Vital parts of a pastor's ministry, such as the selection of church leaders and in-depth counseling, are directly affected by how well he knows the people. A good pastor-to-people relationship doesn't normally happen after only a couple of years.

Think about the implications. Because building trust and developing relationships takes time, a short-term pastor might be tempted to establish programs instead of relationships, to substitute the performance of pastoral duties for developing trust. What you end up with is a pastor with shallow relating skills. And it is this very lack of people skills which will sooner rather than later lead the pastor to yet another move to yet another place of ministry where the chances of his repeating the same experience increases.

8. *There is lack of personal growth.* The church is not only where the pastor works, it is where he grows. A short-termer has little chance to develop a deeper style of ministry. One pastor confessed the effect of his short-term pattern on one area of his ministry—"I do more 'barrel' preaching because of the new work load at the new church." Another short-term pastor admitted, "I have found myself no longer interested in personal development, education or collegiality."

Not only is there a lack of professional growth, but also a lack of personal growth. Bartlett Hess, a pastor in Livonia, Michigan since 1956 observed, "There are many [short-term pastors] who keep running from themselves and their problems, and they should really come to terms."[10] The very pressures and problems God wants to use to bring about growth in our lives, are many times used as excuses to leave too soon, before we give ourselves a chance to grow through the situation to a new level of spiritual maturity.

A modern monk with the vow of stability, Eugene Peterson, once wrote,

> I began to understand my place as a location for a spiritually maturing life and ministry. I saw that the congregation is not a mere job site to be abandoned when a better offer comes

along. The congregation is the pastor's place of ministry . . . but it is also the place in which we develop virtue, learn to love, advance in hope. By providing us contact with both committed and frustratingly inconstant individuals, the congregation provides the . . . conditions for our own growth in Christ.[11]

I could add to this list of disadvantages a few more that have been suggested by other writers, such as the career frustrations that come to a man who develops a track record of short-term pastorates, or the passivity that results in a church from a series of short pastorates, or the increased emotional problems of pastors who stay only short periods of time, or the diminished authority and respect of the short-term pastor in the eyes of the laity. I have heard all of them referred to in one way of another by pastors and laypeople.[12]

But you get the point. Before either a pastor or a church dismisses the idea of the vow of stability, they need to think again. Short-term ministries come with their own price tag— and too many churches and too many pastors have been paying the price unnecessarily for too long.

Endnotes

1. Harry Reader, "Why Most Pastors Are Rehabbers, "*Leadership*, Fall 1987, p. 27.
2. David McKenna, *Renewing Our Ministry* (Waco, TX:Word, 1986), p. 78.
3. Lyle Schaller, *Reflections of a Contrarian* (Nashville: Abingdon, 1989), p. 103.
4. "Shepherds Who Have Stayed," *Leadership*, Fall 1983, p. 138.
5. Lyle Schaller, *Activating the Passive Church* (Nashville: Abingdon, 1981), pp. 57–58.
6. Schaller, *Reflections of a Contrarian*, p. 90.
7. "Shepherds Who Have Stayed," *Leadership*, p. 134.

8. Lyle Schaller, *Survival Tactics in the Parish* (Nashville: Abingdon, 1977), p. 25.

9. Rick Chromey, "Everything I Learned About Ministry, I Learned Dating My Wife," *Leadership*, Summer 1992, p. 21.

10. "Shepherds Who Have Stayed," *Leadership*, p. 142.

11. Eugene Peterson, "The Jonah Syndrome," *Leadership*, Summer 1990, p. 43.

12. This list is suggested from the reading of authors like the following (refer to the bibliography for their works): Ray Ragsdale, *The Mid-Life Crisis of a Minister*; Lyle Schaller, *Activating the Passive Church*; Bill Ligon, C. Peter Wagner and Gerard Gillaspie.

· CHAPTER THREE ·

THE SIDE EFFECTS

Jack (not his real name) and his wife sat across the lunch table from me, asking for help as they sorted through the question of whether or not to leave their present pastorate. We had been friends in college, and a national church conference had given us this opportunity to be together again. When we had first made plans for lunch, I had no idea it would include Jack's wife in tears over the thought of moving.

You see, Jack and his wife had never moved in ministry before! They had never changed churches! The "cloud" had never lifted, the voice had never cried, "Move on!" After 13 years, they were still in the same church Jack had called his first senior pastorate.

After seminary, Jack and his wife accepted a call to be the assistant pastor (with primary responsibilities for youth, of course) at a metropolitan church less than two hours from his boyhood home. When the church started making plans to "mother" a church in a small community north of the city, the senior pastor asked Jack to consider becoming the founding pastor of the daughter church. Jack and his wife said, "Yes."

The first couple of years in the new church start weren't easy. Rented facilities, small numbers and little growth all fulfilled the things that Jack and his wife were told to expect in those early years. Jack had heard from somewhere that the hardest part about starting a church was getting the first 100 people. His church didn't average 100 people until the fifth year.

In his sixth year of ministry, Jack's church faced the decision of whether to take the plunge—to buy land and build. The stress during those days nearly caused Jack to leave. But he stayed. And the church built. During the next six years, the church continued to grow and Jack had to entertain an offer or two to cash in on his successful first experience and leave for another, more established pastorate. Jack said, "No."

Now he was talking to me over lunch about another offer to pastor a church farther west that seemed irresistible. He had gone so far as to send his resume and exchange information with the prospective church. But he was struggling. Should he leave? Should he stay? Was he too comfortable where he was? Was he too afraid to move? This time, Jack was saying, "Maybe."

Our lunch was finished long before our conversation. There were questions that Jack and his wife were asking me that nobody could answer for them. They had to find the answers for themselves. The best I could do was give them some advice and leave them with some things to think about. And among the things I wanted them to think about were the advantages and disadvantages of staying longer where they were.

IS LONGER BETTER?

The answer to this question has varied over the years. One pastor told me about his Bible college professor who taught his class of ministerial students not to stay more than two to three years in any pastorate. The professor explained that "three years was enough, especially when you are young." This kind of advice was fairly common a generation ago.

Even laypeople seem suspicious of long-term pastorates. Maybe they have heard some of the same horror stories that you and I have heard: stories about pastors who "stayed too long," or who "hung on" in their church until they reached retirement; stories about churches falling apart after their beloved and long-term pastor retired, or that went through a string of pastors following a long-term pastor, unable to settle on a successor.

So widely accepted is the fear of long pastorates that there seems to be an unwritten rule that pastors who follow long-term pastorates should not plan on staying longer than a year or two! It is no wonder that clergy and laity alike often question the validity of long-term pastorates.

Even the assumptions of researchers include the underlying belief that longer pastorates are less than advisable. When Allen Nauss measured the relationship of pastoral mobility to ministry effectiveness, he reflected this bias in one of his concluding statements when he wrote, "It was also noted that a very long pastorate of twelve or more years apparently did not affect the effectiveness-rating negatively."[1] While there are some possible negative effects on pastoral effectiveness that come with longevity, as we shall talk about later, it is to Nauss's surprise that he found any effectiveness at all in a longer pastorate. His reaction betrays a preconditioned negative assumption about longer pastorates.

When the research team at the Alban Institute in Washington, D.C. reported their findings in their book, *New Visions for the Long Pastorate,* they admitted their own misgivings about the benefits of longer pastorates. They confessed that when the study of long pastorates was first suggested, they generally felt that "the disadvantages of a long pastorate far outweighed, if not eclipsed the advantages." They were all too familiar with the same horror stories the rest of us have heard, and some we may not have heard:

stories about pastors who were "stuck and locked in by the glutted job market," and other pastors too burned out to think about doing anything—either ministry or moving. These Alban researchers said that they began their study expecting "to find a predominance of such clergy" in their study.

Not only that, but these researchers found out that their negative expectations about long pastorates were reinforced by denominational leaders who were desperate for help to get these long-term pastors "unstuck." Denominational executives, the ones who set policy and supervise pastors and churches, had negative feelings about long-term pastorates, too! To top it all off, the researchers themselves admitted to a "negative bias toward lengthy pastorates" that was an "unexamined assumption." They also admitted to a preconceived opinion that "most long pastorates reflected some defect in the pastor."[2]

Not only was there a question about whether or not a longer pastorate was better, there seemed to be serious doubt about whether or not a long-term pastor was mentally stable! With assumptions like this, who needs enemies, or governing boards?

Recently, thank goodness, some careful study and serious reflection have begun to change people's thinking about longer pastorates. One pastor with a history of shorter pastorates reflected the changing opinions of many when he commented, "My opinions have changed greatly over the years. Now I feel that the long-term pastorate is much, much better."

In their book, *New Visions*, the authors from the Alban Institute state that they were "surprised and impressed early in the study that the majority of the participants [long-term pastors] were in what appeared to be healthy long pastorates." In their report, they reached the conclusion that "while all the disadvantages of a long pastorate can be managed with skill and training, few of the enormous advantages of a long pastorate are available to shorter ministries."[3] I think I hear some minds changing.

If we would just listen to the average person sitting in our congregations, there would be little doubt about their preference for longer pastorates. Lay people that I talked with who have experienced a series of short-term pastors said to me:

> "People in a church generally prefer to see a pastor stay longer."
>
> "Long-term is worth working for. . . . Most people want a pastor to stay longer. . . . It takes three to four years to really get going."
>
> "We just get to the place where we know each other and then he moves on."
>
> "Most of the short-term pastors in our church left too soon."

And what about those pastors who have developed a pattern in their own ministry of short-term pastorates? It may come as a surprise to you, but listen to what they prefer:

> "I am hoping to settle down."
>
> "I wish I had a different pattern of ministry; I don't like short-term."
>
> "I prefer moderate to long-term pastorates over short ones."

On the other hand, we should expect some glowing testimonials on behalf of longevity from pastors and churches who have experienced one or more long-term ministries:

> "I have never felt there was any advantage to a short-term pastorate. I don't like to consider it."

"The four-year term in the U.S. presidency isn't enough! What makes us think it is in the church?"

"I have thought that a long-term pastor was what this church needed."

"I now see the advantages of long-term and I plan to stay."

"I was convinced that long-term was desirable if at all possible. . . . It is best for the person and for the church."

"My feelings for the value of long-term have intensified."

The message from these pastors and churches who have experienced a long-term ministry seems to be, "try it, you'll like it." These comments from clergy and laity on both sides of the longevity aisle only confirm my assumption that pastors ought to stay longer. And churches and pastors need to work harder at what it takes to encourage the vow of stability.

I'VE GOT SOME BAD NEWS

Academic, intellectual and ecclesiastical honesty requires us to take a look at the "bad news" about long pastorates. There is a potential (and I do emphasize the word "potential") downside to longevity. And here are some of those possible disadvantages of long pastorates:

1. *There can be a limited exposure to ministry.* When a pastor and a church have been together for a significant length of time, the pastor's sermons can suffer from a narrow focus, a limited viewpoint and repetition of ideas. This is often caused by a lack of personal growth on the part of the pastor and can result in stunted spiritual growth in the lives of the church members.

Beyond the effect on the pastor's Sunday morning message is the influence that a long stay can have on other ministries of the church. A church with a long-term pastor can suffer in areas of ministry where the pastor is not strong or where he does not place emphasis—unless he develops laity and staff to complement his weaknesses. On the one hand, this results in certain areas of the church's ministry deteriorating (such as children's ministry, outreach, teaching, etc.), while on the other hand, people who have similar strengths as the pastor stand on the side-lines, watching the pastor do their jobs for them.

Not only is the church limited in its exposure to ministry, so is the pastor. Without the exposure to variety in culture, circumstances and places that come with a multi-pastorate experience, it is thought that a pastor can become underdeveloped as a person. Personal and professional growth may be harder. By staying in one church for a longer time, for instance, a pastor can lose his preaching power as he preaches to the same people week after week. In cases like this, his longevity might deprive him of the opportunity to grow from other church situations.

2. *There can be an over-identification of the people with the pastor.* The longer a pastor stays, the more the church people get attached to him. Believe it or not, this can sometimes make it more difficult for him to minister to them. The pastor can become too important to the people, inadvertently developing their dependence on him rather than on the Lord. His long and close relationship with the people can blunt his sermons and he may hesitate to preach uncomfortable truth. He may unconsciously be more concerned about their friendship than their spiritual growth. He may try to please his people rather than risk rocking the boat.

In an interview with "shepherds who have stayed" in *Leadership*, several long-term pastors commented on this danger of over-identification. One senior minister observed, "Another danger [of staying too long] lies in coming to think it is your church." Another remarked, "There are a lot of long pastorates these days that are really personality cults. In fact, one of the greatest dangers of a long pastorate is pride."[4]

A pastor's length of stay and depth of relationship with his people can not only threaten his ministry the longer he stays, it can also make it harder for the church when it comes time for him to leave. Studies have shown that the chances are four out of five that the man following a long-term pastor could encounter problems that may greatly shorten his length of stay.[5]

Even someone like Ben Haden, nationally known pastor of the First Presbyterian Church in downtown Chattanooga, Tennessee, knows this. He once commented out of his own personal experience that usually "the person following such a long-term pastor doesn't last more than eighteen months. The second pastor doesn't last over three years. The third pastor may have a chance."[6]

"In the twenty years I've been here, I feel I've come to know most of you pretty well."

Reprinted from *Church Is Stranger Than Fiction* by Mary Chambers. © 1990 by Mary Chambers. Used by permission of InterVarsity Press, P.O. Box 1400, Downers Grove, IL 60515.

In case you were wondering, Haden's "experience" from which he made this comment was his becoming pastor of the church in Chattanooga. He was following a man who had been their pastor for 40 years! Haden has been there since 1967! Long-term pastorates don't always mean difficulty for the successor.

3. *There can be a gap between the pastor and people.* You might want to accuse me of talking out of both sides of my mouth, but believe me, I am not. While on the one hand people can feel personally close to the pastor as a person the longer he stays, on the other hand, there can develop some gaps in their relationship to him as leader. This "gap" factor seems to be at the center of so many of the concerns about long pastorates. I want to take some time at the end of this chapter to talk about that gap.

Until then, let me tell you that the gap is observable in such situations as the pastor developing his own "entourage," his own following of close friends in the church to the exclusion of others. Sometimes you can see it when the divisions among laypeople are focused on the pastor, or when the pastor begins to lose touch with the congregational mainstream and unwisely objects to new ministry initiatives from the people. He may also suggest ideas that are either out of touch with where the people are or are not broadly shared by the congregation.

Sometimes the "gap" is visible when the pastor ends up doing most everything himself because he thinks it is easier that way and he does it better. Counting on volunteers and being a volunteer from the congregation become unnecessary. Eventually, the pastor takes over the leadership of the church, becoming autonomous, answerable to no one.

All of this talk makes the "gap" sound more like a "great gulf fixed." But take heart. Unlike Evil Knievel's failed attempt to leap the Snake River Canyon on his souped-up motorcycle, this pastor-and-people gap is one that can be crossed.

4. *Ministry can stagnate.* More commonly referred to as "getting into a rut," or "going stale," or "becoming complacent," or "losing flexibility," a long-term ministry can reach a point of boredom. The pastor is heard saying things like, "This is the way we have always done it." And the people lose what little flexibility and openness to change they may have had. The church fails to keep up with contemporary ministry trends and programs. The ministry people in the church stop trying to develop new ministries.

Not only can the church stagnate, so can the pastor. He can lose the sense of challenge. The sense of "sameness" takes over. Fresh ideas tend to threaten him rather than call him to more effective ministry. In his longevity, the pastor can lose sight of his initial goals and priorities.

Pastor Leith Anderson notes that "after pastors have been in a church five or ten years, most programs reflect their ideas or bear their imprimatur. Their schedules are jammed, so they have little time to dream about the future. Momentum shifts to maintaining the program they have built."[7]

A long-term pastor can also begin to think that he "has everything figured out." He can start taking his place and his people for granted. In an honest effort to relieve the boredom, he may find himself becoming overly involved in outside activities. This will leave him with even less energy for the in-church ministry tasks for which he already had reduced vigor. The end result is a church and a ministry suffering from programmatical and spiritual stagnation.

5. *The pastor can experience burn-out.* "Burn-out" was the buzzword of the 1970s. It has hung around long enough to describe the frayed, discouraged and overworked person who has been reduced to either going through the motions or sitting and staring at the wall.

Sitting and staring is what can happen to the long-term pastor who watches the years go by without reaching his goals, who experiences the constant stress and tension of ministry, or whose relationships with his parishioners has become so close over the years that he ends up carrying everybody's burden.

Eugene Peterson once asked himself, "Was it healthy of me to stay in this congregation for so long? Had I taken the place of God for them?"[8] Nobody can play God for very long without burning out!

6. *The pastor and church can feel stuck with each other.* Believe it or not, in a day of rapid-firings of clergy, there can come a point in the stay of a pastor at his church when both he and his church (for differing reasons, of course) feel stuck with each other.

The laypeople might be unhappy with the pastor. The pastor might even be unhappy with the people. Troubled relationships might not be getting any better. Yet the pastor might be afraid to make a change. Or he might overestimate the effect of his leaving on the congregation he has come to know so well. Or he might not want to lose his security. Meanwhile, the church has developed their own sense of security based on their familiarity with the long-term pastor. Neither wants to let go.

7. *There can be reduced benefits for the pastor.* Sometimes, the only way a pastor can improve his financial situation is to change churches. Staying at a low-paying church for a long time doesn't help him provide for his family. And in some church traditions, staying too long in a "low rung on the ladder" church can hamper a pastor's possibility of future pastoral career advancement. Church leaders and colleagues start asking, "What is wrong with him? He has been at that church for a long time. How come?"

And don't think that churches out looking for a pastor don't think the same thing. "There must be something wrong with that man to have stayed in *that* church for that long. He must lack something." A man's vow to stay longer in a less desirable church can sometimes cost him a promotion.

8. *There can be a greater chance of a church split.* Roy Branson has found a correlation between the timing of a pastor's leaving and the number of church splits. Data from a questionnaire he sent out indicates that on the average, church splits occur between the third and fourth year of a pastor's ministry in a church. Using pastoral longevity statistics from the Southern Baptist Church, Branson observed that most pastors leave about the time concerns in the church are reaching a critical point. He concluded that "pastors would have more splits if they stayed longer. . . . If the average stay was ten years, for example, perhaps 75% or more [pastors] would be forced out."[9]

THE GAP THEORY

Now let's talk about that "gap theory" I mentioned a while back. The "gap theory" was discussed by William Hobgood in his unpublished dissertation, "The Long-Tenured Pastorate: A Study of Ways to Build Trust."

Hobgood talks about some of the dangers and risks of long pastorates. In looking for signs of the gap in a long-term ministry, he suggests that we start by asking such questions as: "Does the congregation tend to become homogenous in sociological, theological and value systems?" The inference is that long-term pastorates can create vanilla churches.

Other questions should also be asked, such as:

"Do new programs get generated with as much excitement and energy as in the early years of most pastorates?"

"Are conflicts faced openly and constructively, or are they

avoided?"

"Does the circle of leaders diminish as the years increase, and is power and authority turned over informally to the pastor at points where, in earlier years, it was shared?"[10]

The longer the ministry, Hobgood says, the greater the temptation to become isolated and parochial, the greater the tendency to think self-sufficiently.

More specifically, the gap theory says that "when a pastorate has reached ten years or longer, it will be true that while one-to-one trust between the pastor and *individual* parishioners . . . will be sound and seem to be growing sounder, *corporate* trust . . . will begin to decline, unless preventive dynamics are taking place."[11] Hobgood defines "corporate trust" as the trust between the pastor and the people as a whole for one another.

What this can mean in a longer pastorate is that while the people may trust the pastor as an individual, they still blame him for all the problems in the church. It can mean that what trust there is between pastor and people can deteriorate into pastor and people taking things for granted. It can mean that while the relationship between the pastor and his people may deepen, the church as an organization suffers from lack of professional attention. It can also mean that the more a pastor becomes vested in the inside lives of the people he is leading, the less effective his leadership can become.

In a longer pastorate, power can become centralized and isolated in the pastor. The pastor comes to have a much greater impact on the decision-making process of the church. The power and authority to lead the church are deferred more and more to his opinions and to his circle of friends. Things that used to be done by the whole church, before the people developed love and affection for the pastor, are now done by a few. Without pastor or people realizing it or intending it, the bad side effect of all of that affection and trust between pastor and people can be this centralization of power.

Hobgood goes on to note that the longer a pastor stays, the more likely it will be that the group of people in charge of the church will look like the pastor's choices. The resulting lack of diversity in leadership and key congregational people might explain the slow growth experienced in a number of long pastorates.

In their research, the authors of the study *New Visions for the Long Pastorate* learned that 28 percent of the laity they spoke to mentioned this gap that can develop between a long-tenured pastor and his congregation. In recording their observations, the authors noted that in a long-term ministry, those who dislike the pastor or who disagree with his style will tend to retreat to the edges of the church and wait for another pastor to come along more to their liking. Obviously, the longer the present pastor stays, the longer these folk will wait. Some will get tired of waiting and leave. What they leave behind is a church in which there is a growing number of people who agree with the pastor, creating the possibility of the gap.

While the gap may seem to be unavoidable, it can be averted. Hobgood himself discusses the prevention and correction of the problem. Conscious efforts to share the leadership, to encourage diversity and to delegate power and authority can reverse the potentially harmful and paralyzing effects of the gap in a church's life.

Before you run out and ask every pastor who has stayed longer than four years to resign, remember that this is the bad news. We should know by now that it is always the bad news that gets the headlines. The worst pastor-church stories are the ones that get told the loudest and the farthest. While there are some bad side effects to a pastor staying longer, they are not as bad and not as prevalent as you might think. Especially when we compare them to the more notable and noticeable advantages of having a pastor stay longer.

Endnotes

1. Nauss, Allen, "The Relationship of Pastoral Mobility," *Review of Religious Research*, Winter 1974, pp. 80–86.
2. Roy Oswald et al., *New Visions for the Long Pastorate* (Washington, DC: Alban Institute, 1983), pp. 27–28.
3. Ibid. p. 7.
4. "Shepherds Who Have Stayed," *Leadership*, Fall 1983, p. 140.
5. Lyle Schaller, *Pastor and People* (Nashville: Abingdon, 1973), p. 24.
6. Marshall Shelley and Kevin Miller, eds., "Secrets of Staying Power," *Leadership*, Summer 1986, p. 18.
7. Don Cousins, Leith Anderson and Arthur DeKruyter, *Mastering Church Management* (Portland, OR: Multnomah, 1990), p. 70.
8. Eugene Peterson, *The Contemplative Pastor* (Carol Stream, IL: CT Inc., 1989), p. 157.
9. Roy Branson, *Church Split* (Bristol, TN: Landmark Publications, 1990), pp. 270, 281.
10. William Hobgood, "The Long-Tenured Pastorate: A Study of Ways to Build Trust," Unpublished Thesis, Lancaster (PA) Seminary, 1982, pp. 9–10.
11. Ibid. p. 1.

• CHAPTER FOUR •

THE BENEFITS

Remember the small midwestern church in chapter two that had apparently accepted its role as a "short-term" church for rookie pastors? Let me tell you the rest of the story.

Once again, one of those Bible college graduates landed in their pulpit fresh out of school. He was young and green. Tom (not his real name) looked just like all the other wanna-be pastors who had gotten their start at the "First Church of the Doormat." He was greeted with all the fellowship meals and ceremony that the small church had gotten proficient at putting on through their years of revolving door pastorates.

Only Tom was different. He didn't know about revolving doors. Or doormats. He hadn't told anyone else but himself and his wife that he didn't want to be here in one church for a few years and there in another church for a few years and then on to still another church for a few years. Tom had come to stay in this church longer than anyone else had ever stayed—much longer.

After four or five years, the people began to act a little nervous. What was going on? Shouldn't Tom have left by now? They even started to pull away from Tom, fully expecting him to leave their small church for something bigger and better in the denomination. Still Tom didn't leave. They began to drop hints about his leaving. Not that they wanted him to leave; it was just that they didn't know how to act with a pastor who was planning on staying.

Tom observed all this. Behind their not-so-subtle questions that betrayed their pessimism as to how long they could keep a pastor, he saw their need. This small, struggling church needed someone to stay longer. They didn't need another pastor to flirt and run. They needed a pastor willing to make a commitment to stay longer. Tom wanted to be that man.

So he stayed. And stayed. And stayed. That was over 17 years ago. In the meantime, this small church in an even smaller town started to think better about itself. People in the community began to take notice that the same pastor was still there. Feelings of stability and security started to grow. And so did the church.

As the church began to feel better about itself, its energy for ministry was rejuvenated. It started attracting new people (which is not easy in a town of under 3,000). When the old sanctuary was close to capacity, Tom's commitment to staying longer helped the people feel confident enough to plan for the future. The church purchased land just outside the city limits. A few years later, they built a new facility and relocated, leaving a "downtown" church building that was almost 100 years old. By this time the church had quintupled in size.

Don't you just love happy endings? I don't need to tell you that this church isn't the "first rung on the ministerial ladder" anymore. It has traded its doormat for a welcome mat. It is a vibrant, established, effective church in a part of the midwest that values effectiveness and stability. None of this would have happened if it weren't for a vow Tom made to himself almost 20 years ago—the vow of stability.

I'VE GOT SOME GOOD NEWS

While there are potential trouble spots in pastors staying longer (as we saw in the last chapter), the good news is that the advantages far outweigh the disadvantages:

1. *There is an opportunity for deeper ministry.* In some churches, the pastor is treated more like a visiting relative or a traveling medicine man than one of the family or the tribal chief. He is perceived by long-time church members as simply "passing through." He is just visiting for a few years until something better comes along. He is a "gypsy pastor."

A church and its pastor go through cycles in their relationships. With a long-term ministry, a people and their pastor can go through them together, deepening their mutual relationship and building trust and confidence. It takes time for people and pastor to let down their masks, accept each other, and reach a point where they can work and grow together.

In reflecting on this relational advantage of a longer pastorate, Haddon Robinson said, "Obviously, one advantage of a lengthy ministry is that the pastor has a better chance to bring perception and reality together. The long-term pastor is judged more on his pattern of behavior than on a specific appearance. People are more likely to say, 'The pastor not only talks love; he gives love. He was there in our family crisis when we needed him.' A pattern of care can cover a multitude of less-than-stellar sermons."[1]

Time strengthens the relational bonds between pastor and people as they work through issues and problems in their relationship and in the ministry of the church. As each issue is successfully faced, they experience the joy of developing new relational skills, something more churches and pastors need but never develop.

The longer a pastor stays, the greater the opportunity he has to go through life and family cycles with his people, to get into the fiber of his people's lives and hearts, and make his ministry more effective, more personal and more meaningful. The pastor and the people can watch each other mature. The pastor is there as the children of the church grow up. The pastor can be more familiar with the gifts of his people and more effectively encourage their involvement in ministry. While the pastor may or may not have more of an impact on the corporate decisions of the church the longer he stays (remember the "gap theory"?), he will become a more trusted person and friend and consequently have a greater impact on the personal decisions his people make.

Longevity also affects the pastor's impact in the community. He can make better use of community ministry resources, become more involved in his community's opportunities for service, and have more influence in local civic concerns.

Time is often the missing ingredient in the relationship between pastor and people. In his observations on communicating the Christian faith in one's own culture, missiologist Charles Kraft noted, "Prolonged involvement of person with person assures intensive and effective communication of a multiplicity of messages transmitted and received both consciously and unconsciously concerning a multiplicity of topics. The less personal the communicational interaction, the more the communicational event is likely to devolve simply into a performance."

Kraft goes on to say that while a lot of information might be sent in a less personal communicational relationship, the permanent impact is likely to be low, "owing to the reduction in the person-to-personness [sic] of the situation."[2] A longer pastorate makes possible a better "person-with-person" environment for ministry, whether it be in the church or in the community.

2. *There can be more effective pastoral leadership.* The pastor's leadership level grows only as the people learn to trust him—and this takes time. Larry Osborne, pastor of North Coast Evangelical Free Church in Oceanside, California, writes, "When a pastor finds, as I did, that some of the lay leaders don't want him to lead, it usually indicates that they see him as an outsider, a hired hand to take care of spiritual chores. . . . Let him suggest a change in direction, and he'll quickly learn how little real leadership he's been granted. . . . Until the leaders are convinced it is as much my church as theirs, they will not let me function as their leader. . . . To overcome this, pastors need two things: time and a personal commitment to that local body."[3]

Leith Anderson, pastor of Wooddale Church in suburban Minneapolis, tells the story of his early days of pastoral leadership at Wooddale. He had requested that the church purchase a baptismal robe for him costing about $70. His request was turned down. Thirteen years later, in the midst of a large building program, his request for a change in the layout of the platform was granted without question—even after the concrete had been poured for the original design!

"A dozen years before I couldn't get a seventy-dollar baptismal robe, and now, while a building was partially constructed, they were willing to change it," Anderson writes. "That's because they have grown to trust me. The manager of any organization needs to understand that it takes time to win authority that allows for significant change."[4]

In addition, certain styles of ministry leadership are more effective only if the pastor stays longer. In considering the "equipping/enabling laity-centered" philosophy of ministry as opposed to the pastoral staff-centered approach, Lyle Schaller says that it normally requires at least a 15-year pastorate to install and institutionalize a laity-centered ministry.[5]

Church leader R. Paul Stevens believes that it takes at least six to 10 years for the pastor to fulfill the equipping part of that particular approach to church ministry.[6] And Pastor Bill Hull says that the "disciple-making pastor" needs to realize that this style of ministry takes longer to develop and requires a long-term work.[7]

Part of effective leadership is getting and setting the church's vision for ministry. Early in a pastorate there is usually little time for dreaming and "window-gazing." More pressing and practical tasks call for the pastor's attention. The people want their pastor to be concerned about the everyday matters of ministry.

But with time comes the opportunity and privilege of dreaming. Leith Anderson asks, "How much time ought a pastor

"I still say the new church is a monument to the pastor."

Reprinted from *Off the Church Wall* by Rob Portlock. © 1987 by Rob Portlock. Used by permission of InterVarsity Press, P.O. Box 1400, Downers Grove, IL 60515.

devote to dreaming of the future, especially with a multitude of immediate concerns?" He replies, "The answer varies with each situation, obviously, but much of the answer is determined by how long a pastor has been with the current congregation." He goes on to note sadly that the natural tendencies of ministry pressure and longevity patterns work against a church's ministry having effective vision.[8]

The longer a pastor stays, the better he knows his people. The better he knows his people, the better he can lead them.

3. *The church can be stabilized for ministry.* The longer a pastor stays at a church, the greater the chance for lay leadership to stabilize. People who feel most comfortable with the pastor's style of ministry become the pool from which lay leadership is selected.

Another advantage is that over time, the pastor will not need to introduce major changes—most of the needed change he will have already implemented. Fewer changes means less conflict, and less conflict means greater stability. Greater stability means better conditions for effective ministry. Pastors who stay longer have a greater chance at giving their church stability. William Hobgood reported that 90 percent of the pastors he studied claimed that church crises happened less often in the later years of a longer pastorate.[9]

When talking about the effect of pastoral longevity on the stability of the church, it is interesting to note the importance of longevity on the issue of congregational diversity. Lyle Schaller suggests that the greater the degree of racial diversity in the church membership, the more disruptive are changes in ministry staff. He sees longer pastorates as an important part of the strategy to make a church's diversity work for them rather than against them. While congregational diversity has the potential to be unsettling, the commitment of a pastor to the stability of a longer pastorate can be part of the solution for a racially inclusive church.[10]

One of the reasons why churches with pastors who stay longer can grow is because they don't have to spend their time worrying about what will happen when their pastor leaves. And the reason they don't have to think about that is because their pastor considers their particular parish to be a lifetime calling. They are not always looking around for greener pastures. They are not regularly asking themselves the de-stabilizing question, "Could it be that my ministry here is ending?"

4. *The church can be stabilized for growth.* When pastors are coming and going frequently, a church may develop a poor self-image, a questionable reputation in the community and/or a disrupted ministry focus. But when pastors take the vow of stability, several important ingredients in the life of a church can be stabilized: ministry style, church leadership, community image and ministry vision. When these things are comfortably in place, a church has a better chance to grow.

Because most large churches can point to a long-term pastor at the top, it is a temptation to see pastoral longevity as just another means to the end of church growth, rather than something to be valued on its own merits. The truth is, the kind of environment most conducive to church growth is best produced when pastors stay longer.

In interviews and visits with pastors and laypeople, I have received reports of average churches growing from 25 members to 225, from 200 to 375, of one church mothering another church, and of a Sunday school and church doubling in attendance. And these pastors and lay people tell me that one of the important dynamics of their growth was the stability and continuity in the pastoral staff.

New members are assimilated much more quickly in a longer

pastorate. New people tend to identify with the pastor's style, and because the pastor has stayed long enough for the membership to either accept his style or leave for another church, the new people are more like the "kind of people" already in the church. They have a common acceptance of the pastor and the church's ministry under his leadership.

It is easy to point to the mega-churches and mention the length of time their pastors have been there, but mega-churches are not the norm for most of us. Few churches will grow to the mega-church size, but the growth that can occur in a church is enhanced by stability in pastoral leadership. Just ask your local banker. Part of church growth is church building and bankers are more willing to lend money where they see stability in a church. And when they see a pastor staying longer, they see stability.

After studying churches for more than three decades, Lyle Schaller concluded, "while there is no evidence to prove that either long pastorates or expansion of the program staff will produce numerical growth in a church, there is very persuasive evidence that suggests that it is rare to find a growing congregation that has sustained its growth over a long period of time that has not had the benefits of both long pastorates and an adequate program staff."[11]

5. *The pastor can experience personal growth and satisfaction.* With a longer pastorate comes the challenge to dig deeper. A four- or five-year "barrel" of sermons won't do. A pastor who commits to staying longer is also committing himself to developing new study and work habits as he teaches and re-teaches old truth in a fresh way. He is also committing himself to breaking through whatever four-to-five year ministry patterns he may have developed in previous pastorates. All of this stretches the pastor and calls him to personal growth.

Even in a pastor's first years of ministry, there is a greater benefit to staying longer than leaving early. In a study by Nauss and Coiner of men in their first church after seminary, the authors concluded that "stayers" seemed to provide more benefits for their people as well as deriving more benefits for themselves than did the "movers."[12] The advantages of stability for both the pastor and the church can begin early in ministry.

Scott has been ordained for 15 years. But he is a short-term pastor, lasting less than five years each in three churches. The problem? He says he starts out great, but about two years into his pastorate he begins to wonder, "What do I have left to say? What do I have left to give?"

He has used up the sermons he has already written and covered the basic points of doctrine he always covers. Then he begins to get restless. No church has asked Scott to leave. They like his warm spirit and easy way with people. It is just that he gets antsy about every three years. He is suffering from what James Berkeley calls "stunted growth." He is a "ministerial midget."[13] He hasn't yet accepted the challenge of stretching and personal growth that comes with staying longer.

While this stretching can be difficult, it is also rewarding. No one in ministry really wants to spin his own cocoon. Though some may do so out of their own frustration or lack of energy, no one in ministry really enjoys petrifying early.

This means that a minister may change from topical to expository preaching, from becoming acquainted with people to shepherding them, from performing to pastoring, from going through the motions to going on to maturity.

It also means the pastor has the chance to grow in his areas of weakness, to grow through adversity and prosperity. One pastor notes that the urge to change churches frequently strikes on "blue Monday mornings" when pastors are tempted to move for all the wrong reasons. Among the wrong reasons he gives for moving is frustration over plateaued church growth, a problem with a person in the church, the offer of a better paying position or our own hurt feelings.[14]

Staying through the tougher times gives a pastor the chance to practice what he has preached about such things as handling conflict, the development of the fruit of the Spirit and relating to the difficult people in your life.

In an article in his church paper, one pastor stated that in having to stay and deal with problems he normally would have left behind, he learned new ways of coping, of working through his problems.[15] As another pastor told me, "It brings maturity to know that I have to live with what I have planted."

6. *The pastor and his family can settle down.* On the practical side, there are some family and financial benefits to longer pastorates. Equity in a home, security for the wife, roots in the community for the children—all are positive perks of longevity.

Pastors like to look on the bright side of all that moving around—"We get to see new places and meet new people, my kids love it,"—but we haven't told the truth about the effect of frequent moves on pastors and their families. The truth is, kids don't like all that moving—they put up with it. Good clergy parents can help their kids deal with it correctly. But that doesn't mean moving every three or four years is any less unsettling.

SO WHAT?

What does this all mean? Is longer better? What about those advantages of a shorter pastorate? And what about those horror stories and disadvantages of longer pastorates? We can't ignore them either.

We won't. But let me wrap this up with a few comments, taking everything from the last three chapters into consideration.

First, short-term ministries carry the benefits and liabilities of frequent changes while long-term ministries provide the benefits and liabilities of stability. For some people, frequent change carries a minimum of threat and pain, but for most of the pastors and laypeople with whom I talked, this was not the case. The stability offered by a longer pastorate provides a more secure environment for the other changes which a church needs to be making for the sake of effective ministry.

Second, a long-term pastorate allows for a developing relationship between a pastor and his people that is essential for meaningful pastoral care and leadership. As we will see in the next chapter, the pastor-to-people relationship is crucial for pastoral ministry. And a short-term pastorate does not provide sufficient time for a relationship to develop.

Finally, it has been my observation that short-term pastorates generally produce immature pastors and churches. When a pastor leaves as soon as he begins to experience (or, in some cases, initiate) the first stages of church conflict, he short-circuits the opportunity for his church and himself to grow through the experience.

Usually a pastor leaves as the pressure builds, and the church must wait for a new pastor before they can continue working on the conflict. Meanwhile, the former pastor carries to the next church a short-term pattern of ineffective problem-solving. He stands in his new pulpit encouraging his people to work through relationships biblically, while he has not stayed long enough in one place to do so himself. He is asking his people to apply truths he himself has never learned. Why should they? The only example they have seen is that of pastors walking away from their own people problems. The cycle is then perpetuated. Short-term pastorates breed immature pastors who in turn breed immature congregations.

There are clear advantages to staying longer. The pastors and their wives involved in the Alban Institute study of long pastorates agreed that there was "a clear sense that the advantages of a long pastorate outweighed the disadvantages."[16]

The researchers themselves concluded that "in spite of the potential liabilities of a long-term relationship between pastor and congregation, we remain convinced of the great potential advantage of long pastorates. . . . Virtually all of the disadvantages of a long-term pastorate can be surmounted, yet few of the advantages are available to clergy who remain in a congregation for only a short period of time."[17]

Others who have taken the time to look at the issues of pastoral longevity reach similar conclusions. Nauss, after some study, assumed a negative value for very short pastorates.[18] Gillaspie believes that churches and pastors need to be made aware of the implications of both short and long-term pastorates. He is convinced that once churches and pastors can begin to appreciate, and better yet, experience the "happy results of longer pastorates, they will plan for such."[19]

I couldn't agree more. And neither could Lynn Anderson, minister from Abilene, Texas who writes, "Longevity in ministry is an enormous plus." He says that after nearly 15 years with the same church, he has observed something like this: "The first two years you can do nothing wrong. The second two years you can do nothing right. The fifth and sixth years of ministry, either you leave, or the people who think you can do nothing right leave. Or you change, or they change, or you both change. Productive ministry emerges somewhere in the seventh year or beyond."[20]

Remember Jack from chapter three? I left that dinner and church conference not knowing what Jack and his wife would decide. All I knew was that he and his wife thanked me for helping them talk about their thoughts and feelings and for giving them some things to think about as they considered whether or not to stay longer where they were.

Several months later I heard from Jack. He had said "no" again. He would be staying longer where he was. This makes at least three times during his present pastorate when he has faced the decision to move or to stay. Each time he has chosen to stay. And because he has chosen to stay longer, some good things have happened in his church and in his life.

The stability he brought to the church by staying longer has given the church the confidence to build, and build again. It has resulted in a continuity of ministry and staff. And it has given the church, its ministry and its pastor respect from the surrounding community. It has given his family a place to grow up, and a place for support in times of family need. It has given him a place of acceptance where he can change and grow, professionally and personally.

Jack's church is located in what most suburbanites would call a small town, but at this writing, Jack's church is averaging over 400 on Sunday mornings, has added staff, and is making plans to break the "400 barrier." And his wife doesn't cry over the possibility of leaving anymore. Is pastoral longevity worth it? Just ask Jack. Just ask his church.

Endnotes

1. Haddon Robinson, "What Authority Do We Have Now?" *Leadership*, Spring 1992, p. 29.
2. Charles Kraft, *Christianity in Culture* (Maryknoll, NY: Orbis Books, 1980), p. 149.
3. Larry Osborne, *The Unity Factor* (Carol Stream, IL: CT Inc., 1989), pp. 64–65.
4. Don Cousins, Leith Anderson and Arthur DeKruyter, *Mastering Church Management* (Portland, OR: Multnomah, 1990), p. 50.

5. Lyle Schaller, *The Seven-Day-A-Week Church* (Nashville: Abingdon, 1992), p. 105.
6. R. Paul Stevens, "People in Print," *Leadership*, Fall 1985, p. 98.
7. Bill Hull, *The Disciple-Making Pastor* (Old Tappan, NJ: Revell, 1988), p. 29.
8. Cousins, Anderson and DeKruyter, *Mastering Church Management*, p. 69.
9. William Hobgood, "The Long-Tenured Pastorate: A Study of Ways to Build Trust," Unpublished Thesis, Lancaster (PA) Seminary, 1982, p. 26.
10. Lyle Schaller, *Reflections of a Contrarian* (Nashville: Abingdon, 1989), p. 21.
11. Lyle Schaller, *The Multiple Staff and the Larger Church* (Nashville: Abingdon, 1980), p. 57.
12. Allen Nauss, "The Relationship of Pastoral Mobility," *Review of Religious Research*, Winter 1974, p. 95.
13. James D. Berkeley, *Making the Most of Mistakes* (Waco, TX: Word, 1987), p. 45.
14. Lynn Anderson, "Why I Have Stayed," *Leadership*, Summer 1986, pp. 79–80.
15. William Hulme, Milo Brekke and William Behrens, *Pastors in Ministry* (Minneapolis: Augsburg, 1985), p. 135.
16. Roy Oswald et al., *New Visions for the Long Pastorate* (Washington, DC: Alban Institute, 1983), p. 29.
17. Ibid. p. 74.
18. Nauss, "Pastoral Mobility," p. 80.
19. Gerard Gillaspie, *The Restless Pastor* (Chicago: Moody, 1974), p. 18.
20. Anderson, "Why I Have Stayed," p. 79.

CHAPTER FIVE

BIBLICAL MODELS

"Reverend Eusebius!" It sounded so good. A successful early church pastorate in Rome at last. When he arrived, one of the members of the church was using a bucket of white paint to remove the name of Eusebius' predecessor, Quartus.

"Is it hard to erase the memory of his name?" Eusebius asked the church sign painter.

"Oh no," he said. "This is third time I have painted out a pastor's name in this decade."

"Did you like Quartus?" Eusebius wasn't sure he wanted to ask.

"Was he a good pastor?"

"Yes, but he crossed Coriolanus . . . I heard that his daughter wanted to be a deaconness and Quartus refused."

Eusebius said nothing but swallowed hard. The sign painter continued. "Quartus wasn't really his name, you know. His name was Cato, but it gets easier to call your pastor by a number rather than by his name. Tertius came before him."

"What was his real name?" Eusebius wanted to know.

"Can't recall . . . he only lasted seven months."

"Thrown to the lions?" Eusebius asked, almost preferring that Tertius had been devoured by lions rather than by Coriolanus.

"Nope, that would have been easier! No, we all heard that Coriolanus didn't like a certain sermon Tertius preached against rich Christians who tried to buy pre-eminence . . . he picked an unfortunate text for his sermon."

"What?" Eusebius queried.

"Thy money perish with thee."

Eusebius swallowed even harder. *Maybe I should have gone to Arabia,* he thought to himself.

When he had regained his composure, he said, "Seven months, huh? What happened to the pastor before him?"

"Secundus?"

"Yes, Secundus."

"Well, let's see. That was the split led by Demetrius because Coriolanus wanted to be the moderator and . . ."

"Secundus preferred otherwise," Eusebius finished.

The sign painter look at Eusebius and asked, "How did you know? Do you have the gift of prophecy?"

"No," Eusebius replied, "But I can sometimes see trends."

"Trends?"

"Never mind," Eusebius continued, "Just tell me about Quartus, my immediate predecessor. How did he escape Coriolanus' struggle to have his daughter elected a deaconness?"

"Well, he looked very tired just before the business meeting when he would have been ousted as pastor. He was solid on the point—he would not permit Coriolanus' daughter to be 'crowned.' He wanted out. He was tired of the church and Coriolanus' congregational briberies. So he went through a big crowd on the Lupercal (city plaza) singing hymns to the praise of Christ."

"That was foolhardy!" Eusebius interjected. "Was he arrested?"

"Immediately, and thrown to the lions the very evening the church met to consider his dismissal. Things being what they were, some considered it a nice way to go to be with our Lord. Many of Coriolanus' camp said it was a coward's way out, but Quartus was not much of a fighter, I'm afraid."

By this time the sign painter had painted out the name of Eusebius' predecessor. As he walked away, Eusebius asked him where he was going.

"To the marketplace to get another container of whitewash. You can't afford to get low on white paint in this church. I've got to keep the sign in good shape—all the names current."

Eusebius was disenchanted as he saw the painter walk away. *I have been most popular here in my first few weeks. Surely I have nothing to fear*, he thought to himself. *The fates of Secundus and Tertius and Quartus will never be mine*, he reasoned.

As the sign painter was almost out of sight, he turned back and called out to Eusebius, "Eusebius, will it be all right if I call you Quintus?"[1]

OF MODELS AND MEN

While the concern of pastoral longevity may not be directly addressed in the Bible, the issues surrounding it are. As Calvin Miller has humorously suggested in his *Philippian Fragment*, pastors and churches have had trouble staying together since very early in church history. Yet we don't have much material at all from the first century of the church about pastoral longevity. There are very few models.

It is normal for those of us in the church to look to Scripture as a sourcebook for ministry, but we hear precious little said from the Bible about models of longevity. And since a lot of what we do—in ministry and in the whole of our Christian life—is influenced by models, maybe we ought to take a look at what the Bible might add to our discussion of the vow of stability.

"IS LONG-TERM BIBLICAL?"

That is what one pastor asked me in response to a question about longevity. And it is a good question. We live in a day when the social sciences often claim to have the last word about human behavior and institutions. But the church and the clergy are not simply another human institution. And we dare not settle for having our ministerial behavior take its final cues from sociological research.

A few years ago when the church growth movement was in its infancy, it tended to get much of its direction and reach many of its conclusions from a great reliance on field studies and other methodology related to the social sciences. While sociology can explain some things, it cannot tell us the most important things about the church and a pastor's ministry.

In response to this dependence on social research, Peter Mc-Quilkin wrote the book *Church Growth and the Word of God,* a timely and well-received critique that enhanced discussion about the church growth movement and helped to focus its research.

Compared to the church growth movement, studies dealing directly with pastoral longevity are minuscule. Yet, just like the church growth movement, in the absence of a biblically informed approach, secular models and assumptions presume to fill the void. It is time for a biblical perspective.

In their workbook designed for the pastor-parish committee of a local church, the Lutheran Church in America reminds us that some problems in our understanding of church ministry are the result of the church simply borrowing instruments and procedures from business and industry. Such an approach, they say, will not work. What is missing is the "theological why" and an "understanding of the nature of ministry." Further, borrowing such research instruments often results in forced attempts to compile statistics on things which cannot always be treated quantitatively.[2]

What we need is a good look at what help the Bible can give us in building our understanding of pastoral longevity. While the following discussion of a biblical perspective on pastoral longevity is by no means comprehensive, it will provide us with some structure and impetus for further development of the themes, biblical models and principles related to long-term ministries.

As we begin our look into biblical models of ministry, we recognize that the styles of leadership in the Old and New Testaments are not exact correlations to contemporary ministry. Our understanding of professional ministry is different today than the formal and informal ministries of Scripture.

While the subject of pastoral longevity is not directly addressed in Scripture, the general concerns of leadership and ministry longevity are present. In some cases, ministry longevity is implied while in other cases, general biblical principles for ministry from the Scriptures are applicable to the issues of longevity.

In this chapter, we will look at models of ministry in the Old Testament, and in the lives of the two most prominent ministry figures of the New Testament, Jesus and Paul. In the next chapter, we will take a closer look at some biblical themes and principles that relate to our study of longevity.

GIVE ME THAT OL' TESTAMENT LONGEVITY

The earliest models for leadership and ministry in the Old Testament come from the patriarchal structure of society. The father of the tribe or clan was looked to for family decisions and final blessings. Abraham, Isaac and Jacob, well-known figures of Genesis history, headed their families from manhood until death. In their cases, "longevity" was for life!

This patriarchal model later developed into tribal leadership positions such as the "elders" of Israel. Though there is no direct reference to the length of term for service for these leaders, the earlier patriarchal model would imply a time of indefinite and lengthy tenure in leadership.

Then comes Moses, called by God as the first national leader for enslaved Israel. He was not appointed by God for a specific length of time, but rather to a specific task, to "bring my people the Israelites out of Egypt" (Exodus 3:10).

Moses did not know how long the task would take or when it would end. If he had, maybe he would have objected more strongly at the burning bush! Because of his own disobedience, God put a limit to his service, not allowing him to enter the Promised Land. But it was the people's disobedience that stretched the length of Moses' ministry. A task that should have taken no longer than a year lasted 40 years in the wilderness!

Following Moses, Joshua was called to complete another chapter in the life of God's people. He was to take all the people and "cross the Jordan River into the land I am about to give to them" (Joshua 1:2). Joshua and Moses both served in their leadership positions until their death. As each became the chief leader of his people, it was apparently assumed he would lead for life.

The next stage in Old Testament ministry leadership was the period of the judges. Called by God at strategic points of need in the life of God's people, their influence over their countrymen usually lasted a lifetime. The pattern can be seen in Judges 2:18–19 where we read, "Whenever the LORD raised up a judge for them, he was with the judge and saved them out of the hands of their enemies as long as the judge lived. . . . But when the judge died, the people returned to ways even more corrupt than those of their fathers." It seems that even back then they had trouble adjusting to life after a long-term leader!

In his introduction to the Old Testament, Roland Harrison presents two chronological tables for the judges. In one, he lists 12 judges spanning the years from 1376 B.C. to 1051 B.C. with an average length of service for the judges of 27.1 years. In the other, using H.H. Rowley's *From Joseph to Joshua* as his source, the average length of ministry for the judges is 34.2 years.[3] No matter which table is used, the ministry and leadership of the judges was a long-term involvement with the people of Israel.

Following the period of the judges, Israel was ruled by kings. These military, political and spiritual leaders were recognized as "God's anointed." Their leadership ended only by natural or involuntary death (assassination, war, etc).

While the literal use of the years of service for the kings may be open to some question (the number "40" may have signified a long period of time rather than exactly 40 years), the impact of the numbers is still the same. Forty years is a long time whether it is taken literally or figuratively. We get the message either way.

The first three kings of the united nation of Israel averaged 40 years of leadership. With the division into the two kingdoms, north and south, longevity among the kings decreased. The indictment of the prophet Hosea indicates that longevity was becoming impossible because of the undisciplined times. He accused the people of plotting the new king's assassination on the night of his inauguration (Hosea 7:5–7).

Using estimated figures supplied by Harrison, the average length of service for the kings of the Northern Kingdom was 10.4 years. For the kings of Judah (Southern Kingdom), the average length of service was 18.1 years.[4]

PROPHETS AND PRIESTS

Prophets and priests are the remaining models for ministry and leadership in the Old Testament. These two ministries are the closest Old Testament equivalents to the New Testament church office of pastor-teacher. The prophets had varied backgrounds. Some came from priestly families. Others came right off the farm. Still others attended the Old Testament's version of seminary, the prophets' school.

While some prophets served for life, others had short ministries. A few were called by God to deliver a specific message at a particularly important time in the life of God's people. Some prophets preached their message in their own countries, others to foreign nations, and a few crossed between Judah and Israel (Northern and Southern Kingdoms).

While the judges, kings and patriarchs were perceived as "one of us," the prophets stood outside the national circle and addressed it as a third party. Rather than being appreciated as national deliverers and leaders, they were accused of being traitors and doom-sayers.

Because scholars don't agree on the prophets' lengths of service, there's no way to accurately figure the average length of their ministries. Some lasted no more than a year or two; others lasted 40 years or longer. Could it be that these erratic patterns of the prophets' ministries bare a resemblance to the erratic patterns of ministries today?

On the other hand, the priests reflected a more stable ministry. Numbers 4:3 says that the Levites (priests and assistant priests) served terms of service beginning at age 30 and lasting until age 50, when they would semi-retire to train younger priests. Not much later, the age of entry into the priesthood was lowered to include five years of apprenticeship (Numbers 8:24–26). And still later, the beginning age was lowered again to 20 (1 Chronicles 23:24). The priesthood was a hereditary position passed on from father to son, reflecting the patriarchal pattern. Examples of this father-to-son lineage can be found in First Chronicles 6:4–15 and 9:33–44.

The longevity of the high priest is uncertain. For instance, Hebrews 7:3 says that the "former priests existed in greater numbers, because they were prevented by death from continuing." But by the era of the New Testament the high priest was tenured. Roland DeVaux, in his book on ancient Israel, says that biblical chronology "gives exactly twelve generations of priests from the building of the temple under Solomon to its reconstruction after the exile . . . and . . . exactly twelve generations from the making of the tent in the desert to the building of the temple."[5] This information gives us a maximum average length of service for the high priest as 40 years—a generous estimate at best.

Following the exile, there were 28 high priests between the years 37 B.C. and 70 A.D., with an average length of service of 3.9 years! This figure reflects the tremendous discontinuity in spiritual leadership brought on by the upheaval and corruption in Israel at the time. The priestly system became corrupted; spiritual confusion among the people was encouraged by a number of pseudo-messiahs who found people ready to follow them anywhere.

As you may have already noticed, the 3.9 years average tenure for a high priest after the exile is very similar to today's average length for pastors to stay in one church! Could it be that this modern discontinuity in spiritual leadership reflects some "upheaval and corruption" in today's churches and contributes to the "messiah complex" of ever-moving pastors? These pastors are wanting people who will follow them. At the same time, we have "messiah-seeking" congregations who hope that the next pastor will be just what they are looking for!

These models of Old Testament ministry serve as an interesting background for what we will find in the New Testament. These patterns of longevity are informative and perhaps even a bit inspirational. While they do not directly affect the ministry of today's pastor, they do suggest a style of leadership and service that is founded on longer-term relationships.

OUT WITH THE OLD, IN WITH THE NEW

Some people get nervous when we begin studying biblical models and principles for church ministry in the Old Testament. It could be because they are less familiar with the Old Testament, or they aren't sure how applicable those models are to the New Testament church. They should feel a lot more comfortable when we take a look at the models and principles of longevity in the New Testament.

When we do take a look, disappointment awaits us again. Longevity is not specifically addressed in the New Testament either. However, there are plenty of New Testament principles and models for ministry that indicate the appropriateness of longevity in ministry.

But we have another problem when we start to look at the New Testament and longevity. The New Testament has no well-known models of pastoral longevity. This is because of the timing and nature of the New Testament books. Conservative estimates of dates for the books of the New Testament do not allow enough time for longevity patterns to develop. Many of the early church leaders did not begin their ministry in the churches of Asia Minor and Greece until the time of Paul's ministry in the mid-50s A.D. If the bulk of the New Testament (excluding Revelation) was written before the fall of Jerusalem (70 A.D.), you can see why there would not have been much said about longevity. In addition, there were a lot of other more pressing issues to address in the first-century church, such as persecution and heresy.

The New Testament books zero in on gospel proclamation. The history of the church's early years is mainly written by itinerant ministers in letters to established churches and church leaders. Most of the churches weren't in existence long enough to have any long-term leaders. The office of pastor wasn't as firmly established or as readily recognized in the first century as it would be by the middle of the church's second century. References to longevity in the letters to these churches are found in general instructions to church leaders, not in personal examples.

JESUS AND LONGEVITY

The earthly ministry of Jesus Christ is certainly no model of longevity! His public ministry lasted just three and a half years. Some even estimate that Christ's ministry was only one and a half to two years. Yet Jesus could say at the conclusion of his ministry, "I have brought you glory on earth by completing the work you gave me to do" (John 17:4).

While his statement reflects a task-oriented approach, he maintained an excellent balance between tasks and people in his short ministry.

Jesus commissioned his disciples twice to short-term ministry: first the 12 disciples in Matthew 10 and then the 70 disciples in Luke 11. He must have known the truth of the statement "familiarity breeds contempt" when he himself was forced out of Nazareth after an all-too-brief ministry there. "A prophet is not without honor except in his home town," Jesus said of the incident in Matthew 13:57. Longevity appeared to be impossible for Jesus, especially among people who knew him best.

Jesus' ministry was finished when he had accomplished what

he came to do. In another sense, though, his ministry is still going on: "But because Jesus lives forever, he has a permanent priesthood. Therefore he is able to save completely those who come to God through him, because he always lives to intercede for them" (Hebrews 7:24–25).

When the resurrected Christ renewed Simon Peter's call to ministry in John 21, he used the shepherd as an image of ministry. Three times Christ commissioned Peter to "feed my lambs," "take care of my sheep" and "feed my sheep."

Jesus used the same image when referring to his own ministry as the Good Shepherd in John 10. Peter's final impression from Christ about ministry was "shepherding." This image influenced Peter's life and the ministry in the early church (1 Peter 5:1–3). It ought to influence ours as well.

The shepherd image of ministry does not allow for a changing of flocks very often, but rather implies a relationship developed with the sheep through years of contact that enhances the shepherding and thus the life of the sheep.

While Christ's earthly ministry is considered "short-term" according to our standards, and the disciples' mission during Jesus' earthly life even shorter, we must understand the "specific task" of Christ's ministry. There is room for short-term ministries for specific, difficult tasks that can best be accomplished in the short-term. Jesus had just such a ministry.

We should also not use the disciples' ministry trip as a model for anything other than what it was—a time for in-service training. Some short-term ministries are designed for specific tasks. Jesus' own short-term ministry was for one of those "specific tasks" especially tailored for short-term tenures. As we saw in an earlier chapter, such specific-task ministries are fewer than what is often claimed. And by the way, you will not find most advocates of short-term pastorates also favoring crucifixion as a method of removing the pastor!

There can be no argument that Jesus' earthly ministry was short-term. And while there are many ways that Christ's ministry is a model for our modern ministries, his three and a half years should not be the norm for us today.

PAUL AND LONGEVITY

Paul's ministry was that of a traveling missionary, not a local church pastor. He was called to a specific task that took him to faraway places. Paul understood his own calling as being a priest to the Gentiles (Acts 22:15; Romans 15:16).

While Paul's ministry was "here a little, there a little," he understood and encouraged principles of ministry that would lead to longer stays (we will take a look at some of them in the next chapter). He also experienced some of the problems and frustrations of a short-term pattern.

Paul's pattern of longevity in ministry was a direct result of his call. He purposely planned for short stays in various locations (Romans 15:19–24; 1 Corinthians 16:5–6; 2 Corinthians 1:16). His short-stay pattern was not only intentional, it was reproduced in the lives of two of his protégés, Timothy and Titus (1 Corinthians 16:10–12; 2 Corinthians 8:19).

At times, Paul's "long-distance, short-term" ministry pattern created its own difficulties. It caused people to be confused about his real intentions for ministry to them (2 Corinthians 1:16–17). It complicated the problems at Corinth when it appeared that Paul left too soon (1 Corinthians 1:11; 5:1). Several times he had to revise travel plans to visit a troubled church he had left after a short ministry (2 Corinthians 12:14, 20; 13:1).

His short ministry at Corinth was not only not long enough to baptize many, it also wasn't long enough to deal with the quarrels and divisions that developed after he left (1 Corinthians

1:14). Short-term ministries and premature ministry termination did not solve or prevent church fights in Paul's day, and still are not as effective a solution to keeping the peace in church differences as some think for today's church.

Task-oriented people, like Paul, have a different idea of "closeness" in relationships than people-oriented persons. They also have a different idea of how long it takes for that closeness to develop. Paul considered the Corinthians his "work in the Lord" (1 Corinthians 9:1) and even called himself their "spiritual father" after only one and a half years of ministry (4:15). It is obvious, however, from the defensive posture of Paul throughout both of his Corinthian letters, that this was more his feeling than theirs. He may have felt the bond after a year and a half (7:3), but they didn't.

It seemed that Paul was not always aware of how people less task-focused than he was were affected by their brief exposure to him. Several times Paul's letters encouraged churches to imitate him (1 Corinthians 4:16; 7:8; 11:1; Philippians 3:17; 4:9; 2 Thessalonians 3:9–10). But this is hard to do when the man you are trying to imitate didn't stay around to model for you! It's hard to remember what he was like after such a short ministry. Paul's quick entrances and exits only seemed to intensify the problem (1 Corinthians 4:17).

Those to whom Paul did minister seem to have remembered the content of some of his teaching (1 Corinthians 11:2) more because of his follow-up letters than because of his short ministry with them. Much of his ministry to people occurred through these letters. He even admitted that writing was part of his strategy. He was even sought out for advice by the churches he had helped to start (7:1; 2 Corinthians 13:10; Ephesians 3:3–4; Philippians 3:1; Colossians 4:16).

Paul did not seem to be as affected by his short ministry stops as his constituents were. Paul saw letter-writing as a valid and valuable teaching tool in his absence, as useful as mouth-to-ear communication (2 Thessalonians 2:15). From Paul's perspective, his verbal instructions and written advice were one and the same. There should have been no confusion (2 Corinthians 13:2).

The problem was, however, that while Paul may have felt free to express himself in writing (2 Corinthians 6:11,13), such writing allowed for the people to whom he was trying to minister to read between the lines (2 Corinthians 1:13; 5:9–11). So instead of clearing up the issues left hanging when Paul left them after a short time, his letters seem to sometimes confuse and sadden the readers (2 Corinthians 2:1–5; 7:8) Often the people don't appear to know Paul well enough to interpret the tone of his letters (2 Corinthians 10:1, 9–11).

Though Paul gave similar directions to several of his churches (1 Corinthians 7:17), it is dangerous for a short-term pastor to carry his personal agenda from church to church, even when the churches appear to be similar. It does seem, however, that by carrying his personal plan of starting churches, teaching basic doctrine and addressing current ethical questions to the churches in which he ministered, Paul brought to each church some initial stability and continuity (1 Corinthians 11:16).

The problem was, Paul's early exits and ministry "in-absentia" left him dependent on hearsay for personal care and pastoral correction (1 Corinthians 1:4, 8–9). Sometimes he seemed to prefer it that way, afraid of what he might find if he were to come and visit them (2 Corinthians 1:23; 12:20–21). Then there were the times when he wanted to be "person with person" with them but was unable (1 Thessalonians 2:18; 3:2).

Still, there were times when Paul was realistic about the limits of his pattern of ministry. He knew the effects it might have on people. He realized that there were some things he could not do in a short-term or "in-absentia" ministry that he could most certainly accomplish in person (Philippians 1:17; 2:12; 4:3; 1 Thessalonians 3:10).

Though Paul was confident and comforted that God could work in the lives of his people even after he left them (Philippians 1:6), he once expressed a desire to visit a church and to stay there for a longer time (1 Corinthians 16:7). Paul knew, in spite of his own short-term style, the importance of staying (Philippians 1:25).

If Paul's pattern of ministry tells us anything, it tells us that short-term ministry can create its own set of problems. But it also tells us that all is not bleak for the short-term minister. Even in short-term ministries, Paul experienced deep and bonding relationships. For example, in Acts 20:18–38, the people's attraction to Paul was not affected by his short-term stay with them. They responded to his integrity and sense of personal

"Dear Timothy, I'm sending under separate cover, extra copies of the spiritual gifts inventory quiz for your church."

investment in them while he was with them.

What is interesting to note about the affection expressed by the church leaders of Ephesus to Paul is that Paul's ministry at Ephesus lasted three years, the longest stay of any of his ministries (Acts 20:31). Paul seemed to have a similar attachment with the people in Galatia (Galatians 4:5). For Paul, short-term ministry did not mean that he was less concerned about the needs of people (Philippians 2:20). It just meant that he had to express it in a different way.

Paul's longevity pattern indicates that he was a task-oriented, goal-oriented person. When he was done with a specific short-term task in each city (which in most cases, was starting a church), he looked for another challenge. Although Paul claimed to be present in spirit when he was absent in body (Colossians 2:5), the people were not always satisfied. They were wishing that his body would have stayed longer.

Jesus and Paul both were short-termers. And both of them seemed to understand the limits of their short-term ministry. Yet beneath the surface statistics of their short ministry patterns are some important, foundational principles for a longer ministry.

ON THE ROAD AGAIN

So far, we have used people in the "professional ministry" as subjects for our biblical study of longevity—the Old Testament kings, priests and prophets, Jesus and Paul. Before we move on to some biblical principles which apply to pastoral longevity, I would like to introduce you to two laypeople who were anything but long-termers in their church experience. And they have more in common with the mobile American of the last decades of this century than you might imagine.

Aquila and Priscilla are models of mobility. From the research that is available, we can piece together their story. Aquila, from

Pontus in the northwestern part of Asia Minor, married Priscilla. Some time later, they moved to Rome.

Expelled from Rome in A.D. 49 with the rest of the Jews, they moved to Corinth for a couple of years. There they met Paul, shared a tent-making business with him and then moved with him to Ephesus. While they lived in Ephesus, the local church met in their home. After Paul left Ephesus, they stayed long enough to invest themselves in a young preacher named Apollos.

What happens next is a bit unclear, but it appears that Aquila and Priscilla moved back to Rome once more and then back to Ephesus for the last time.

In spite of all this moving around (it makes today's pattern of pastoral longevity looked sedentary), they committed themselves to the local church in each place they lived. Paul praises their commitment when he commends them to the church at Rome. They had endangered their lives for him.

Their commitment in the midst of mobility is an example to mobile Americans who all too frequently stop attending a church after a move, or refrain from getting involved in a local church because "they are going to be here for only a couple of years." Short-term ministry does not have to mean shorted-out ministry.

Endnotes

1. Calvin Miller, *The Philippian Fragment* (Downers Grove, IL: Inter-Varsity Press, 1982), pp. 20–23.
2. *Mutual Ministry Workbook* (Philadelphia, PA: Division of Professional Leadership), p. 1. (Manual o.p. Updated version: George E. Keck, "Staff Support Ministry" Chicago: ELCA, 1988.)
3. Roland Harrison, *Introduction to the Old Testament* (Grand Rapids, MI: Eerdmans, 1969), p. 178–179.
4. Ibid. p. 735–736.
5. Roland DeVaux, *Ancient Israel—Religious Institutions, Vol. II* (New York and Toronto: McGraw-Hill, 1965), p. 375.

CHAPTER SIX

BIBLICAL
PRINCIPLES

One of the things I didn't tell you about Tom in chapter four is that he is a PK (preacher's kid). All through his childhood, he had lived in the parsonage, listened to his dad preach and moved when his dad moved.

It was the moving that affected Tom the most. When he graduated from Bible college, took his first church and decided to commit himself to that church for a long-term ministry, it was in part a reaction to the constant moving his pastor-dad had put the family through when Tom was a boy. By the time Tom entered the ministry, he had decided that while he could admire his dad for most everything else, there was one thing he did not want to emulate: he did not want to be a career short-term pastor.

Tom had seen short pastorates up close. And while he may not have seen any clear examples of longevity, he knew that somehow longer pastorates had to be better than what his dad had experienced.

Maybe it was Tom's own inner desire for security and settledness which he had never felt as a child that led him to take the vow of stability. Or maybe it was something even deeper, perhaps a conviction based on some principles of ministry gleaned from God's Word. More than likely, it was a combination of both. While no one else can benefit from Tom's personal desire for stability, we can all develop similar convictions about longer ministries from some very important biblical themes and principles of ministry.

RELATIONSHIPS AND RECONCILIATION

Two of the most important biblical themes about ministry that encourage longevity are the scriptural principles dealing with relationships and reconciliation. As we take a closer look, you will see how they can be called upon to support the case for longer pastorates.

Let us start with the principle that ministry occurs best in the context of relationships. Several times Paul mentions the relationship between minister and people:

> You know how we lived among you for your sake. . . . We were gentle among you, like a mother caring for her little children. We loved you so much . . . you had become so dear to us. . . . For you know that we dealt with each of you as a father deals with his own children. (1 Thessalonians 1:5; 2:7, 8, 11)

Again and again in the New Testament we see the issue of a believer's relationship to another believer presented (and assumed, I might add) as the context for ministry. For instance, referring to the early church's ministering elders as "shepherds" suggests the dynamic of knowing the "sheep" longer and better. A minister who knows people in-depth over a longer time is in a better position to speak to the harder issues and minister in the sticky situations in life.

In Paul's letters to his young believers, he directs them to minister to one another in more than 20 different ways (love one another, honor one another, encourage one another, pray for one another, etc.). This kind of believer-to-believer ministry can best occur when there are relationships between people.

Lyle Schaller writes that one of the keys to being an effective pastor is "to survive the trials and tribulations of a pastorate long enough to build relationships with people that constitute an essential part of the foundation for reinforcing and expanding the total ministry and outreach of that congregation."[1] Long-term relationships between pastor and people create the potential for effective ministry.

When William Hobgood talks about the importance of relationships in ministry, he uses the word "bonding." This is what he says must take place between the pastor and his people in order for meaningful ministry to occur. He observes that the personal trust between a pastor and his people does not happen easily, frequently taking years of hard work to develop. "Though the office of pastor will help it happen," Hobgood writes, "it will not, finally, become a reality until time has passed and the pastor and people have lived through the times of life that demand that relationships become more than mere acquaintanceships and more than formal role-taking."[2]

How important is this "bonding," this relationship quotient to a longer pastorate? Hobgood offers his opinion that a pastor will not be able to stay much beyond eight years in one church with any sense of hope and joy in his ministry unless this bonding has taken place with a majority of the people in the congregation. "The long pastorate is characterized, more than anything else, by a two-way street of trust and intimacy between the pastor and parishioners."[3] That's spelled r-e-l-a-t-i-o-n-s-h-i-p-s.

A second theme that bears significance for longer pastorates is Paul's favorite doctrine of reconciliation. For Paul, reconciliation is at the heart of the gospel message. It speaks of a restored relationship with God, once broken by the sin of one party and now restored without violating the standard of God's holiness. Paul writes that in order for our relationship with God to be made right, God makes us righteous with the righteousness of Himself. (2 Corinthians 5:21). Reconciliation means a restored relationship which can be enjoyed by both sides.

Christ was the original agent of man's reconciliation to God. "God was reconciling the world to himself in Christ" (2 Corinthians 5:19). He didn't just proclaim that reconciliation. He illustrated it in his life and ministry. And it showed up in His relationships to those with whom He came in contact. Reconciliation isn't just an abstract doctrine, it must be a person-to-person experience.

There are some immediate implications of the theme of reconciliation for ministry and longevity. After restoring man's relationship to Himself, God assigned to man the job of passing on this message of reconciliation (2 Corinthians 5:18–20). But remember, reconciliation is more than a verbal message. To be most effective, it must be acted out. Paul used phrases like "ambassadors" and "God [is] making his appeal through us" as well as pointing to the example of Christ as the earthbound agent of God's reconciliation. What this says to us is that reconciliation is best proclaimed when it is evident in the life of another human being.

Reconciliation is a gospel truth that is to be lived out in relationships. When the man who sinned in Corinth (1 Corinthians 5) was dismissed from the church and subsequently repented, Paul asked the church to restore the man with forgiveness (2 Corinthains 2:5–10). In so doing, they would be allowing him to not just hear the message of reconciliation, but to experience it on a personal level.

Relationships as a context for ministry and reconciliation as the acted-out message of ministry are best developed in a longer rather than a shorter ministry. While a short-term ministry allows for a correct (and effective) verbal presentation of the message of faith, it may not give sufficient opportunity for people to see that message fleshed out in the life of the messenger. On the contrary, too many times, rather than seeing reconciliation acted out by the pastor, the people of the church see the man leave in the heat of battle, unable to handle or heal broken relationships. If, as Marshall McLuhan has said, the "medium is the message," then we need to ask ourselves, what message are we sending by our shorter pastorates? Which medium is better able to communicate the truths about relationships and reconciliation?

Relationships and reconciliation are the "R and R" of ministry. Relationships establish the environment within which the message of reconciliation can be experienced. Both are important biblical themes upon which a man should build his ministry. Both ask that a pastor and a church think about staying together longer.

CAN YOU PICTURE THIS?

The New Testament is a gold mine of theological word pictures. It begins with the illustrations of spiritual truth in the parables of Christ and in Paul's word pictures, continues with the symbolism of the Jerusalem temple (Hebrews 7–10), and ends with the colorful visionary portrayals of divine truth in John's Revelation. It is in the nature of spiritual truth that it is best communicated in stories and images.

Throughout the New Testament, a number of these word

pictures refer to the church and its ministry. We learn about the church from such metaphors as "body," "bride," "flock" and "nation of priests." All of these word pictures have implications for the church's ministry.

For example, Gillaspie, in speaking of the image of the church as a "flock" and the pastor as "shepherd," says that one of the reasons for "unreasonably brief" pastorates is the faulty conceptions we have of the essential nature of what a pastor is and does. "If the whole duty of a pastor consisted of preaching," he argues, "then he might change his field of service continually without loss." But if, as Peter (1 Peter 5:2) says, the pastor is a shepherd of souls, and, as Gillaspie points out, "each year increases his effect on lives," then these ties between pastor and people (shepherd and sheep) "cannot be broken easily without some hurting effect."[4]

There are other word pictures of the church and its ministry that have a direct impact on how we think about longevity. Let's put up the easel and take a look at some of them.

THE CHURCH AS A FAMILY

People in 20th-century America don't need more institutional programs or more professional staff. What they need, says Tom Sine, are "small groups, 'families,' where people are known and loved—where they can find healing, discover God's kingdom vocation for their lives, and be empowered to reach out in love to others."[5] The church has the potential to be that kind of family.

It was the Apostle Paul who likened the church to a family. In two of his letters, he used the word "household" like we would use the word "family" (Ephesians 2:19; Galatians 6:10). The Greek word is *oikeios*, which means "belonging to a house, being a family member." The family picture of the church is reflected in Paul's references to his "fathering" the Corinthians (1 Corinthians 4:15) and in his speaking to his churches as to his "children" (1 Corinthians 4:14; 2 Corinthians 6:13; Galatians 4:19; etc.).

Paul writes using the same kind of family language when he talks about being "in the pains of childbirth" for the Galatian believers (Galatians 4:19). He tells the Corinthians that he has fed them with milk (1 Corinthians 3:2), and he likens his ministry to the church at Thessalonica to that of a "mother caring for her children" (1 Thessalonians 2:7), making yet another comparison of the family experience and the church. A

"Not one of the last ten pastors has been able to get along with us."

Copyright 1979 Larry Thomas. Used by permission.

bit later, Peter picks up the same family-nursery theme to talk about his ministry to new believers (1 Peter 2:2).

In Paul's personal instructions to Timothy, the elder states-man of the traveling apostles pinpoints the similarity between ministry in one's own family and ministry in the church family. He tells the young Timothy, whose youthfulness appeared to be a problem for him in his ministry (1 Timothy 4:12), to relate to others in the church as he would to family members—like sisters, brothers and fathers (5:1–2). "Timothy, treat the church as if it was a big family," I can hear Paul saying.

The implications of this image of the church as family for ministry in general and for long-term ministry in particular are clearly and dramatically expressed by Juan Ortiz. He says that while a "club can change presidents each year by election," a church should "never change pastors, because it is a family; and the pastor should be the father." This thought-provoking churchman goes on to ask us, "Whoever heard of a family that changed fathers every other year, or of a father who ran off and left his family to take on another, larger family?"[6]

While Ortiz's statement leaves no room for pastoral transfers and may leave us feeling a little uncomfortable, the image of the church as family does introduce a sense of stability to a very unstable longevity pattern in the American church. And don't think that the people in our churches don't have a family feeling about their church. One layperson said to me, "Pastoral changes are analogous to a father and children changing every couple of years; both the pastor and church suffer."

The image of the church as family and the minister as parent shouldn't bind a pastor to his place of ministry, but the con-sideration of this image should give us a new appreciation for the value of longevity and the relationship between pastor and people.

THE CHURCH AS A FIELD

In First Corinthians 3:9 Paul refers to the church as "God's field." He uses the term *georgion*, found only in this passage in all of the New Testament. In their margin, the translators of the New American Standard Bible offer the alternative reading, "cultivated land." Others see a veiled reference to the Old Testament image of Israel as the vineyard of God (Isaiah 2; Luke 13:6–9).

In the context of the First Corinthians 3 passage, Paul is using the process of cultivation to talk about his ministry. He talks about his part of the ministry being that of planting, about Apollos' part in the watering, and God causing the growth. He makes a special emphasis that the one who plants and the one who waters work together: "The man who plants and the man who waters have one purpose," he writes, "and each will be rewarded according to his own labor" (3:8).

In applying this picture of the church as God's field to the issue of pastors staying longer, I would like you to think about several points of application. First, it is God who appoints each minister to his work (3:5). Beyond the politics of the denomination or the pressures of the pastoral search committee, the man and the church involved need to acknowledge that God is in charge of the process. Or is He? Too many times the calling of a pastor to take a church sets the stage for an early exit.

Second, each minister has his own labor and each man's labor has its own intensity, its own type and its own length of service in the field. The reality of the work of farming is that each part of the work takes different amounts of skill and time. Planting, cultivating and harvesting are not the same tasks, and are not meant to be accomplished in the same amount of time. It takes only a couple of weeks at the most to plant and harvest, but months and months to grow a field.

Each pastor needs to understand his part in the overall work of God in growing a church to maturity. While some men can stay through the work from planting to harvesting, others may be better at one or two of those tasks. In saying that, we need to remember that the normal pattern, taken from the "farmer in the field" metaphor, is for a man to stay through at least one cycle from planting to harvest, however long that might be.

Third, each minister did what the circumstances called for. One planted, another watered. In focusing on the issue of pastoral longevity, or on any issue of ministry, it is often easy to make that one concern the most important issue of all. This third insight about longevity from the church as a "field" helps us to understand that pastors and their longevity are not the only focus. Pastors staying longer is a good goal, but it is not the only end in sight. Pastoral longevity is still only a means to an end, the harvesting of God's church.

THE CHURCH AS A BUILDING

In the same passage where Paul refers to the church as a field, he calls the church "God's building" (1 Corinthians 3:9–11). In his letter to the Ephesians, he calls Jesus Christ the "chief cornerstone" and refers to the church as "being built together to become a dwelling in which God lives by his Spirit" (Ephesians 2:20, 22).

The writer of Hebrews picks up this same word picture for the church and compares the church to a building which is better than the building of Moses, who had an important part in building the Old Testament people of God (Hebrews 3:1–6).

It seems that of all the word pictures and metaphors of the church, this one was a favorite beyond the first century of the church. In the post-biblical writing, "The Shepherd of Hermas," the author talks at length about the "building of the tower" as a picture of the building of the church.

If the church is like a building, then it only follows that members of that building should be busy "building up" one another. And that is exactly what Paul says is the responsibility of every believer (Romans 14:12; 1 Thessalonians 5:11). The building up of oneself was not to be the primary focus, not even in the exercise of one's spiritual gifts (1 Corinthians 14:12, 26). Everyone's effort was to be directed at building up the "building of God."

This activity of "building up" became a checkpoint for a man's ministry in the church. Even Paul, with his apostolic authority, was to use his position to build up, not tear down (2 Corinthians 10:8, 13:10). And since Paul saw his ministry primarily as that of "foundation laying" (1 Corinthians 3:10; Romans 15:20), he expected anyone following him to be a builder of the building of God as well.

While Paul does not carry this image of the church as a building any farther, I believe we can make some safe applications of this picture of the church to ministry, especially as it concerns our focus on longevity.

First, both the "field" and the "building" images suggest that there are natural places to terminate a ministry. Neither image would lead us to conclude that there is never a time to leave a place of ministry. The initiation or termination of a pastoral ministry, however, should be done with a consciousness of God's call (1 Corinthians 3:5) and with full consideration of the gifts of ministry that God has given a man (3:10).

Second, whatever decision is made about staying or leaving a place of ministry, the underlying motive and eventual outcome needs to be the "building up" of the church. This does not mean that people talk themselves into "what is best for the church" and then make a warped decision. All too frequently I hear either pastors or people say "it was best for the church for me/him to leave" when what they should have honestly said was, "It was the easiest and most convenient thing to do." When we look at the church as a building, "up-building," to use the word of noted Pauline scholar J. Christian Beker, ought to become an important factor in any church decision.[7]

Third, an incoming pastor ought to apply the "building" metaphor by asking himself, "What kind of building is this church? What stage in its construction is it? Am I acquainted with its very unique architecture, its setting and surroundings? Can I add at least another layer or story in keeping with its design? Does it need strengthening in its foundation or basic structure? Will I commit myself to staying long enough to build with continuity? Do I have the skills that this building job calls for right now? How many stories could I help build?"

A helpful concept comes from Lyle Schaller, who encourages pastors to think of staying at a church in terms of "chapters." He suggests that pastors ought to think of their ministry at a particular church as a series of chapters or terms rather than as a block of so many years. "By looking at a pastorate in terms of stages of ministry rather than the passage of time, the pastor is encouraged to think in terms of what is happening rather than how long he has been there."[8]

Schaller's "chapters" correspond to the "stories" of a church "building" that a man might build during his years of ministry in a particular church. Schaller goes on to say that a pastor may experience many chapters (stories in the building) in one church.

He adds, however, that any one effective chapter may not last beyond three or four years in length, creating a need for a pastor to consider writing another "chapter" in the life of the church rather than settling for a shorter term of ministry. If a pastor is to write a series of chapters in the life of the church, what he must fight against is what Schaller calls a "vocational depression." This "down-time" in a man's ministry seems to coincide with either the third to fourth year, or the end of the second (or sometimes the third) "chapter" in that pastorate.

Schaller advises, "If this [vocational depression] can be seen as part of the normal pattern and if the pastorate can be seen as a series of chapters, it may be helpful for the pastor to ask, 'Am I really at the end of this pastorate here, or is this merely the conclusion of one chapter or am I trying to identify the theme and outline of the next chapter?' "[9]

Whether you think about a pastor's ministry as "stories" in a building or "chapters" in a book, the length of a pastor's stay in one pastorate can be enhanced if both he and the church would begin to think of their working together as one chapter, one story at a time. As each story or chapter nears completion, instead of developing a sense of "it's over," there can be a sense of "I wonder what the next chapter will be about?"

HERE COMES THE BRIDE?

Many of the pastors and church people I speak to about the issue of pastors staying longer compare the relationship between the pastor and people to that of marriage. They say it in a number of ways:

> "I like the marriage concept of pastoring."
> "To suggest to a pastor that he ought to leave is like saying to a husband and wife that they ought to get a divorce."

For all their good intentions, I have some very bad news for pastors and people who talk like this. Marriage is never used as a model for the relationship between a pastor and his people. It is only used as a picture in the New Testament of the church's relationship to Christ as His "bride" (Ephesians 5:25, 27). Let me say it again. Marriage is not a biblical model of a pastor's relationship and ministry to his church.

In fact, the use of the marriage model in ministry can be harmful. First, it can be harmful to the church people and their expectations. In referring to the pastorate as a marriage, one layperson commented, "I look upon the pastor's leaving like a divorce—with all the grief, the hurt, the guilt. There is trauma each time a pastor leaves."

Second, the marriage model can be harmful to the pastor, his relationship to the church and his own marriage. While one "wife" is his by marriage, the other "wife" is his by ministry, and we all know what happens when a man tries to keep two wives happy—just ask Jacob, Eli or Abraham! Spiritual polygamy is no more acceptable than actual polygamy.

The marriage metaphor, though popular, cannot and should not be applied to the pastor-church relationship, and should never be used as a motivation for longevity. Commitment for all of life comes in only one earthly relationship: between husband and wife. The pastor-people relationship should not demand such a commitment.

I would suggest that instead of using the marriage model as the commonly accepted paradigm for the pastor-parish relationship, we use the "family" model: not with the pastor as the "big daddy," but as a person with many spiritual brothers and sisters—some older, some younger.

As a pastor relates to those in his church as members of his family, it increases his motivation to stay longer—and when he does leave, the transition is not accompanied with the negative feelings of "divorce." There may be sadness, but there won't have to be guilt and anger. Instead, everyone can celebrate the time they had together and look forward to future reunions.

READING BETWEEN THE LINES

As we have seen, longevity may not be commanded in the New Testament, but Scripture encourages it through its principles and implications. It is difficult to build a case from Scripture that would do anything other than encourage pastors and people to stay together longer for the sake of ministry, for the sake of the church. It just feels right.

Biblical allusions and implications are not the same as direct

"Here we go, the return policy."

teaching, but they must not be ignored. If you read through the New Testament epistles with pastoral longevity in mind, you find implications throughout. You may want to do your own study, but these are some of the insights I've gleaned from my own reading of the letters of the New Testament:

1. The longer a person knows the people among whom he ministers, the greater the potential for ministry (Romans 1:12; 2 John 5).

2. A longer association between people and leader is a more meaningful setting for the application of the instructions about their relationship (Romans 12:10; 1 Thessalonians 5:12–13; 1 Timothy 3:7; 5:17, 22; Titus 1:5; James 3:1).

3. Principles about ministry gleaned from the ministry of Christ as our High Priest are enhanced in a longer term ministry (Hebrews 5:2; 6:1).

4. Many of the leaders of local churches in the early church were chosen from among their own people, who must have known these leaders for some time in order to accept them as leaders. Their longer relationship made their leadership more acceptable (2 Peter 2:1; 1 John 1:3; 1 John 2:19; 2 John 10).

5. One of the benefits of a longer association with people is the opportunity to make comments about relationships with a greater degree of credibility (2 John 12; 3 John 13).

6. And finally, there is a place, on occasion, for shorter ministries! (3 John 8).

Further discussion of these and other New Testament verses as they relate to longer ministries can be found in Appendix A.

THE CHURCH FATHERS AND LONGEVITY

What happened to the church in its second century of ministry? By the time the church had a chance to develop some observable patterns of longevity, were there any? Is the subject even talked about?

I could find no direct references in post-biblical writings about longevity. There are, however, indirect comments that have implications for longer ministries.

For instance, in Clement's letter to Corinth (paragraph #42), transient apostles were contrasted to appointed bishops whom we can presume were more settled and long-term. People needed to be aware of the difference between short-term and long-term ministries. In paragraph #44 of that same letter, Clement discussed local church leadership, with the assumption that the leaders had been known for some time by the congregation.

In the epistle of Saint Ignatius to the Ephesians (paragraph #9), the dangers of a person in ministry just passing through were stated. The implications are that long-term is preferred and that there is a need and desire to know the minister better than is possible in a short-term relationship.

According to the Shepherd of Hermas (Mandate #11), a man's possession of the Spirit was to be tested by his life, not just by his position. This kind of evaluation could not be done except in a longer relationship.

The Didache (paragraph #13) expresses a preference for longer ministries by noting the fact that there were prophets just recently settling among the people in contrast to the established ministers who had already been settled among the church people for quite some time. The newer prophets were strangers compared to those who had already been ministering for a while. In fact, two paragraphs later (paragraph #15), the Didache refers to those very bishops and deacons who had been appointed from among the people, rather than the new arrivals.

By the second century of the church, there is every indication that Bible teachers in the local church were not expected to move around in the same manner as other traveling ministers, such as the traveling prophets. Instead, these pastor-teachers were to "live among the people, learn of their needs, so that in spite of the standardization of the 'didache' they would be able to treat it with sufficient flexibility to meet the spiritual needs of those for whom they were responsible."[10]

THE BIBLICAL EQUIVALENT

We have heard one skeptic already ask, "Is long-term biblical?" My answer must be that, while no such term can be found in the original languages of Scripture or in any modern translation, no biblical literalist should take comfort in this omission.

The Bible presents us with a picture of leadership among God's people that hardly leaves room for short-term ministry to be considered preferable. From the leaders of Israel in the Old Testament to the principles of ministry in the New Testament, long-term ministries are encouraged.

Jesus and Paul had special short-term ministries because of their unique tasks. Paul's experiences are good illustrations of the frustrations of short-term ministry for most of us, whether we are the minister or the one being ministered to.

Ministry models make the most sense when they are applied to a longer-term ministry. The pastor as shepherd, the church as family, field and building, all suggest a realistic approach to longevity. They also point toward the potential of fulfilling more ministry goals in a longer ministry.

The biblical principles of ministry are perhaps the strongest persuaders of the need for longer pastorates. Relationships are established best, and reconciliation is modeled best in a longer ministry.

Is long-term biblical? Though the term may not be found in

Scripture, its biblical equivalent can be found in the Old and New Testament models and principles for ministry.

Endnotes

1. Lyle Schaller, *Survival Tactics in the Parish* (Nashville: Abingdon, 1977), p. 11.
2. William Hobgood, "The Long-Tenured Pastorate: A Study of Ways to Build Trust," Unpublished Thesis, Lancaster (PA) Seminary, 1982, p. 7.
3. Ibid.
4. Gerard Gillaspie, *The Restless Pastor* (Chicago: Moody, 1974), p. 14.
5. Tom Sine, *The Mustard Seed Conspiracy* (Waco, TX: Word, 1981), p. 160.
6. Juan Ortiz, *Disciple (Carol Stream, IL: Creation House, 1975), p. 97.*
7. J. Christian Beker, *Paul the Apostle* (Philadelphia: Fortress Press, 1980), p. 321–322.
8. Schaller, *Survival Tactics*, pp. 15, 25.
9. Ibid. p. 26.
10. Everett K. Harrison, *The Apostolic Church* (Grand Rapids, MI: Eerdmans Publishing, 1985), p. 166.

• CHAPTER SEVEN •

THE OBSTACLES

A t 35, Ray (not his real name) found himself the new pastor of a large church on the West Coast. Confident of his call to pastor the church, he arrived with dreams to realize and desires to achieve. He was lovingly received by the 1,700-member congregation. His three children adjusted well to their new schools. Things couldn't have been better.

His ministry began to prosper. In response to his preaching ministry, the church began a radio program aired locally and overseas. Other ministries were added in those first two years: a newspaper column and a "dial-a-message" phone line. Ray's ministry seemed to be going well.

Until year three—then the problems started. Because of Ray's seminary and denominational background, some people in the church began to question his integrity, theology and approach to ministry. They sent letters to members of the church and to the overseas missionaries supported by the church.

Eventually, Ray and his wife were called before the church board. Attendance and giving began to decline. There seemed to be a general malaise over the church. People started moving their membership to other churches.

After only two years, Ray felt like quitting. He knew that two years was below the national average for length of pastorates. But with all the problems and pressure, he didn't know how he could stay any longer.

OBSTACLE COURSE

While the specifics may vary, the plot of Ray's story is played out again and again in church after church, usually resulting in the pastor's leaving.

In spite of the desire of most pastors and churches for longer pastorates, they are still the exception, not the rule. Loren Mean, executive director of the Alban Institute in Washington, D.C., paints a familiar picture. "All too often," he writes, "when a pastor takes up a new assignment or call the same frustrating series of events occurs."

First, Mean says, there is a burst of enthusiasm for the new pastor and hope for the church. Then a few things go wrong, dashing some of those hopes, followed by some personal differences that start showing up. These sore spots give old church conflicts a chance to erupt again. Finally, disillusionment sets in and both the pastor and the people start thinking that maybe it is time for the pastor to move on.[1]

This is the anatomy of many short-term pastorates. And the dominant tendency, says Lyle Schaller, is that pastors move too soon.[2] Research indicates that a substantial number of pastors are open to the idea of moving to another church 35–45 months after arriving in a new pastorate.[3] Very early in the new ministry, the seeds are planted for yet another short-term pastorate.

Pastors and churches are faced with the dilemma of wanting something (longer pastorates) that they are not quite sure how to get. While long pastorates have their trials no less severe than short pastorates, just as unfortunate and more frequent is the tragedy of short pastorates that end in the sudden and hasty change of pastors. And many times these moves are made for the most trivial of reasons.

What prevents longer-term pastorates? If everyone prefers them, why aren't there more? The truth is, while they are hoped for, they are not expected. And few people understand what makes a longer pastorate happen. What causes pastors to move? Why aren't there more pastors and churches experiencing the stability of longevity?

It is probably because barriers to the longevity that is so desirable yet so elusive are unknowingly erected by the very people who want longer pastorates. If we could begin to identify some of these roadblocks, pastors may be more willing and better able to take the vow of stability, and more churches may make it possible.

TAMING THE BEAST

This chapter and the next will focus on the greatest barriers to longevity, as identified through study, research, and personal interviews. An old sage once said, "To name the beast is to tame the beast." Once these obstacles to longevity are identified, I believe we can begin to manage them.

I didn't say eliminate them. There will always be some allowable and unavoidable exceptions to longer pastorates. But if more pastors and churches are to take the vow of stability, they need to learn about the pressures they will be facing. After we have finished this course on obstacles, we will spend the final chapters developing some steps to managing them.

Throughout this book, I may have given the impression that longevity is exlusively a pastor/church problem. It may have seemed I was saying, "If only pastors and churches would do something different, the problem of shorter pastorates would be solved."

Actually there are two other participants in the business of creating obstacles to longevity: denominational leaders and educational institutions must bear some responsibility. There are some things they unknowingly do that also contribute to the short-term pastorate pattern.

This is not meant to be an indictment, or to sound antiestablishment. It is an invitation to all members of the team—pastors, churches, denominational leaders and educational institutions—to assist in managing the obstacles to longevity. All four have an important part to play.

OBSTACLE #1: Lack of Awareness

The first obstacle to pastoral longevity is a general *lack of awareness* of the problem. People have either not taken the time to learn or have failed to understand the dynamics and benefits of pastors staying longer.

Pastors

I feel the most important variable in the issue of pastoral longevity is the pastor himself. The other players in the drama—churches, denominational leadership and educational institutions—play their own significant roles, but the pastor is in the best position to know more, teach more and manage better the issues of longevity than anyone else.

Yet many pastors are unaware of the issues surrounding longevity. They may have some vague sense that pastors ought to be staying longer, but they aren't quite sure how. One pastor I spoke with about pastoral longevity, who himself had experienced a series of short-term pastorates, commented to me that my series of interviews had begun to raise the level of awareness about longevity among the other pastors in the district. Before I began asking questions, few men, it seems, in spite of the statistics of short pastoral stays in that district, had given it much thought.

This lack of awareness takes many forms. In some cases, it is just the assumption—by the pastor, the congregation or both— that he shouldn't or won't stay long in one church. Clergy often give each other cues that imply that short pastorates are normal. "Haven't you been there long enough?" they ask each other. "When are you going to move?" is asked in jest. Or is it in jest?

Many pastors think it is abnormal to stay in one church too long, and they become suspicious of colleagues who do. Others refer to a long-term pastorate as "being stuck." Colleagues and denominational leaders start to wonder if the long-termer is using the church as a "ministerial security blanket."

In seminars he has directed for long-tenured pastors, Dr. Donald Freeman, professor at Lancaster Theological Seminary, has had some participants say, "I should move on, but my heart says, 'Why should I move?' " It is as though they were fighting an ecclesiastical or denominational expectation.

From his private counseling with pastors through the years, Robert Schuller reports that "the majority of ministers of all denominations accept the call or assignment to a church with the expectation of staying on only until something better comes along." Most pastors do not come to a church with a "commitment to stay long enough to make it a great church."[4] They don't seem to have given longevity much thought.

Too many pastors enter the ministry or take a church unaware of the forces that work against their staying beyond the four-to-five-year average. Lloyd Rediger, from the Office of Pastoral Services for his state denominational conference, has identified three times in a man's life when he will be most concerned with the issues of staying or leaving. Often these times are more related to stages of his life than to issues in his current ministry.

Stage one consists of young pastors in their first or second church. Stage two commences 10 or 15 years into a ministry career, when a pastor begins to ask, "Is this the way I want to spend the rest of my professional life?" And stage three is about five to 10 years before retirement, when a pastor may begin to wonder if his ministry is going to be all downhill from here on.[5] Each stage brings its own pressure to move. If a pastor isn't aware of some of these tendencies, he may find himself moving when he really doesn't want to—and he may not understand why.

Frequently a pastor will succumb to a "greater challenge" he sees in a new place of ministry. In a survey of clergy in the Lutheran Church, it was found that the majority of clergy tended to explain their acceptance of calls to change churches because it was an "opportunity to be of wider service in a new position," or there was in his present church a "decline in the possibility of carrying out pastoral goals."[6] While new challenges are certainly a part of a legitimate pastoral change, a pastor needs to be honest with himself. Searching for "greener grass" can lead to an unnecessary move.

Pastors who lack an understanding of the values and challenges of pastoral longevity will end up moving too frequently. Once they begin to learn about the benefits and obstacles, they will be more willing to help manage a pastorate toward longer stays. Norm Shawchuck, director of spiritual formation for the United Methodist Church in Indiana, says the bottom line is, "What does the pastor want? Does he want to stay or go? The pastor's own mind is the key to longevity."

Churches and Laypeople

As important as the pastor is, it takes two sides to make it happen. A healthy long-tenured pastorate is the outcome of a joint pastor/people pilgrimmage, which calls all parties to "eternal vigilance" and to a profound mutual caring and commitment to ministry.[7] Yet, sadly, many churches are ignorant of how to make it happen. They profess a desire for their pastors to stay longer, but they too, don't know how to make it happen.

Many churches begin on the wrong foot. Well-meaning laypeople appreciate their pastors, but at the same time send signals that they do not expect them to stay long before they begin climbing the ecclesiastical ladder. Have you ever heard anyone say to their pastor, "I hate to think of it, but one of these days we're going to lose you. You are too big for us. You will go far in ministry, etc."?

One pastor told me what he began to notice after he had been at his church for a couple of years. He could hardly believe what

"He was traded to Valley Church for a music director and a youth pastor."

he was hearing, but his people started teasing him about leaving! Another pastor said that his people were of the opinion (and told him so) that five years in a pastorate was a long time!

It is a widely held assumption by laypeople that after the sixth or seventh year of ministry, a pastor is available to move, regardless of where he is in his current ministry. Churches expect it, act like it and end up planning for it. One pastor said he believes that his people have their own inner "alarm clock" that starts to go off after a pastor has been there for four or five years. Some churches have a short-term pattern that initially was the result of a series of short-term pastorates, but is now the cause. Having known nothing else, they just figure that this is the way it is supposed to be.

I have noticed that the majority of churches that have experienced a series of short-term pastorates had short-term expectations. By the same token, churches that had experienced at least one long-term pastorate were a bit more hopeful that their next pastor would stay a long time. Short-term churches had little basis for such hope.

Many churches also have negative assumptions toward longer pastorates. They sometimes hesitate to call a man who has been at another church a long time. They are afraid to think about getting "stuck" with the same pastor that long. Rural churches see themselves as "stepping stones." Lay leaders act like a long-tenured pastor is a threat to their position and power in the church. Without consciously admitting to it, many churches will not look for or encourage a long-term ministry from any pastor.

After eight years as a youth pastor and assistant pastor, Larry Osborne had finally taken his first senior pastorate. Excited by the challenge, full of ideas, energy and enthusiasm, he was looking forward to the opportunities ahead of him.

Since the chairman of the church board had been in Europe when Larry candidated and was called, Larry made an appointment to see him at his earliest convenience. Meeting at a local pancake house, the chairman greeted him pleasantly and then asked Larry what he had in mind for the church. For the next 30 minutes, Larry shared his dreams and visions.

When Larry had finished, the chairman leaned across the table and said, "Son, don't get too many fancy ideas. You just preach and pray. We'll run the church. And don't dig your roots too deep, either, because it's a good idea to move on every three or four years."[8]

While it is true that most laity assume their pastor will not stay long, their overwhelming secret desire is just the opposite. But the fact is, most churches will never experience a long-term pastorate. Statistics indicate that only one pastorate in 20 is long-term. The short-term expectations of the average layperson appear to be self-fulfilling.

Denominational Leaders

The lack of knowledge and awareness of issues pertainng to pastoral longevity is also endemic to denominational leaders. You would think that the people who are in charge of placing and replacing pastors would want to know all there is to know about longevity. You would think they would be interested in increasing the stability of the churches in their charge by increasing the average length of pastorates. But while they are well aware of the need for improvement, they are all too unaware of what they need to know to help longevity.

Unfortunately, both at the national and district level, denominational leadership frequently ends up a part of the problem rather than part of the solution. Instead of designing programs and procedures to address the concerns of longevity, and engaging in activities to help pastors and congregations become more aware of the issues, they unwittingly help build some of the obstacles to longevity.

Some of the responses I heard from pastors reflect this lack of understanding among denominational leadership. I asked them, "What do you think contributes to short-term pastorates?" Listen to some of their answers that reflect on denominational leadership.

> "The district superintendent was telling young pastors that since this was their first church, they should stay only two or three years and then move on."
> "I wish the district superintendent would leave men alone who have been in a church for a short time."
> "The district superintendent is too quick to jerk a man and replant him. . . . It seems to be the mindset of [this] era to do that."

Just like pastors and churches, denominational leadership lacks an understanding of longevity. They, too, often have negative assumptions about long-tenured pastorates. And they often support the "ladder mentality" among clergy by seeking or recommending the "bright young clergy" for advancements.

Educational Institutions

And finally, there are the educational institutions—Christian colleges and seminaries where future pastors are trained. How aware are they of the issues of longevity? How much information and preparation do they give pastors-to-be about staying longer?

When I asked pastors who were in their first church the question, "What did you learn in your schooling about pastoral longevity?" this is what they said:

> "From college came the mindset of expectation of stepping stone churches, with the first church or two being stepping stones to future ministries."
> "The talk in the college snack shop was about short-term, stepping stone pastorates."
> "None of my classes ever addressed the subject of longevity."
> "We got the non-verbal message that longevity was not a serious possibility."

There were some pastors who had heard of longer tenures when they were in school. But most of what they received in their training taught them how to minister, not how to minister longer. There was plenty of talk about how to candidate, the art of coming and going. This emphasis assumed that students would be changing churches frequently, so they needed to know all about how to leave and get another church. It seems that no teachers spoke of what makes longer pastorates possible or desirable. Students were left to form their own opinions (which, I might add, were probably based on their experiences of a series of short-term pastorates in their home churches).

A quick look at any Bible college or seminary catalogue will reveal a long list of fine, ministry-related courses for people training for the pastorate. The curriculum will include subjects like church-planting, theology of ministry, evangelism, inter-personal relationships, leadership and ministry internship. While some topic areas (such as relationships and conflict resoluton) come close to talking about longevity issues, you are unlikely to find any time given to a study or discussion about how a pastor can stay longer in a pastorate.

Hindrances to longevity are not only in the curriculum, but

in the school's expectations of students. Theological graduate schools "usually reward the kind of student who loves books more than people, who are [sic] highly skilled in conceptualizing abstract ideas, who are strongly task-oriented, who speak when spoken to, who tend to be introverted personalities, and who display a high degree of patience."

Most local churches, on the other hand, reward "ministers who are heavily person-oriented, skilled in interpersonal relationships, excel in oral communication, enjoy one-to-one relationships with people, are competent in both small and large group dynamics, who speak first, and who are gregarious, extroverted personalities, who are skilled initiating leaders, who are willing to take risks, and who are highly productive leaders."[9] While the institution is busy producing one kind of pastor who has not been exposed to the value of longevity, the local church is looking for another kind of pastor whose make-up might help him stay longer.

A major obstacle to longevity occurs even before a pastor takes his first church. During his training, he receives little or no instruction about the value of long-term ministry and its related issues. Educational institutions apparently are not as aware of longevity as they need to be. "Entrusted with the training of future pastors," writes Gillaspie, they "should outline the advantages of longer pastorates and make a strong argument for such."[10]

A Call to Awareness

Everyone—pastors, churches, denominational leaders, and educational institutions—should be more aware of longevity issues than they are. There are plenty of places to go and plenty of things to learn that would help us become more aware of the concerns of longevity. Let me give you just one example: the "white water" period of ministry described by George and Logan.

After the arrival of a new pastor, and after a few years of turnover in membership, a church reaches a point where the number of people who have come since the new pastor arrived equals the number of people who were there before the pastor came. This equality of "newberries" and "formerberries" can create a crisis in the pastor's ministry. George and Logan refer to this time as the "white water" period. The white water period usually takes place between the fourth to sixth year of a pastorate, at a time when the new pastor's future is not yet secure. In fact, George and Logan note: "the fatality rate during this

"Today's sermon is one I've wanted to preach for some time now . . ."

period is so high, that many pastors have a pattern of about four-year pastorates." Where have we heard that before?

The authors comment that sometimes whole denominations show this pattern in their churches. "Churches, pastors, and whole denominations will all benefit from understanding this element of the dynamics of the four-year pastorate," they write—especially since many have observed that a pastor's most effective period of ministry comes after the sixth year.[11] Everybody can learn something more about longevity. Everybody needs to.

OBSTACLE #2: *Lack of Personal Growth*

A second major obstacle to pastors staying longer is the *lack of personal growth* by pastors. "How can a congregation continue to grow spiritually over the years? The most obvious answer is either to have a series of spiritually mature clergy or to have one leader who is always pursuing his own spiritual growing edge."[12] A pastor who is growing personally has a far greater chance of staying longer.

"Some may bring short pastorates upon themselves. The minister who gets caught in the humdrum of life and neglects the essentials of personal Bible study and prayer soon will find himself inadequate for the continuing challenge of the longer pastorate. Such a man may find it necessary to move to another church simply because he is not personally prepared to take his church to greater heights in growth and service. The man who desires the effective longer pastorate must grow."[13]

Those in the professional ministry can avoid boredom and burnout by taking the time to develop themselves. Personal spiritual nurture, professional development, continuing education, all are part of the plans of a pastor who intends to stay longer where he is.

But not many pastors plan for personal growth. They are too busy adding more work to an already hectic and over-burdened work load. Only 20 percent of America's Protestant clergy continue their education with a minimal one week of continuing education in any form each year.[14] If a pastor moves every couple of years, he can avoid having to concern himself with personal or professional development. However, if he is ministering to the same people year after year, he must renew and refresh himself.

In their publication *Ministry Currents*, the Barna Research Group listed seven reasons why pastors change churches so frequently. Two of those reasons deal with the need for a pastor to be concerned with his personal growth.

First, there is the "Peter Principle" of ministry. Sometimes a pastor feels that he has taken the church as far as he can. While he has been a fine pastor, he does not feel able to take the church beyond a certain point to its "full potential"; he must choose to either grow or leave. If he doesn't take some time to develop his leadership abilities, he will end up leaving for another church. There he will once again grow to the limit of his own inabilities.

Second, shorter pastorates are sometimes caused by burned-out pastors. Our society demands more and more productivity with less and less time for personal renewal. "Pastors who demand regular periods of recreation and solitary reflection are viewed as sluggards." It is the workaholic who gets the appreciation. In spite of such attitudes, a pastor must make time regularly to restore his energy and passion for ministry.[15] The alternative is a frazzled, fatigued, frustrated and fruitless minister.

One area of growth that is crucial is leadership. In the research of the Alban Institute into pastoral firings, they discovered that clergy were more vulnerable to firing after the completion of a building program. Failure on the part of the pastor to adapt his leadership style to a new stage in the church's life was cited as one reason for this pattern. During a building program, the focus of the church is specific and the leadership of the pastor is task-oriented. Once the buiding program is over, the congregation needs a new focus and the pastor needs to grow and adapt his approach to leadership. When he fails to grow, he sets the stage for an earlier-than-necessary exit.[16]

If a pastor is wanting to stay longer where he is, he must be ready to make some shifts in his thinking and leading. And that means growing and changing. The pastor who isn't growing won't be able to grow a ministry in one place very long.

OBSTACLE #3: Lack of Self-understanding

Some pastors say they leave for "external" reasons—the church fails to build, fails to hire additional staff or attendance declines. But those around them wonder if there are other reasons. Afraid to ask the pastor what he is *really* thinking or why he is *really* leaving, laypeople become suspicious. Behind this mystical "leading of the Lord" to take another church, are there more pragmatic and personal reasons for the move, such as personality conflicts, desire for a bigger salary, being closer to family or pastoring a larger church? The pastor may not admit it, but the congregation's suspicions may be closer to the truth than either the reasons he has given publicly or those he has voiced in his own heart.

A pastor's decision to leave involves factors within himself of which he may not be fully aware: his leadership style, personality, background, insecurities, dreams, tendencies to be a "stayer" or a "mover." The better a pastor knows himself and the more honest he can be within himself, the better he will be able to evaluate and learn from his reactions to pastoral transitions.

Unfortunately, just like the rest of us, pastors are not always able to know themselves like they should. This *lack of self-understanding* is the third obstacle to pastoral longevity. When a pastor isn't able or isn't willing to understand why he feels what he feels or why he decides what he decides, he is more apt to make poor decisions. Frequently, the decision to leave before he should is made with a lack of self-understanding.

First, there is the understanding of one's own personality and gifts and how they might affect long-tenured pastoring. There do appear to be some clergy whose personality type and skills are better suited for long-tenured pastorates. It is interesting to note that pastors and laity seem to agree as to what those types and skills are. The pastors and laypeople I spoke with told me that the pastor who is a likely candidate for a longer pastorate is someone who can fit anywhere, is a "slow pusher," a people person, dominant but not domineering, versatile and flexible.

When I asked these same pastors and laypeople what leadership and personality type is more likely to be a short-term pastor, they described a person who is a driver, autocratic, rough on people, unwilling to change, forceful, melancholic, and who wants to be put on a pedastal. Anyone care to apply?

In a study of mobility patterns in Southern Baptist churches among the "upwardly mobile" pastors, those likely to settle down in one church to develop a growing ministry, were the best educated, least authoritarian, less charismatic and unorthodox in ministry.[17]

It goes without saying that each pastorate is different. Each pastor's gifts for ministry vary. Which ones are better suited for the long haul? Calvin Ratz suggests that the "person with a teaching-pastoral ministry will tend to last longer than someone whose ministry is more prophetic or evangelistic." To counter this opinion is a study that said shorter pastorates are caused by pastors who may be teachers, but not leaders.

We may not be able to settle the differences here, but the point is this: pastors need to know themselves—their gifts and personality. Knowing these things helps them do what they need to be doing to make a longer ministry possible. I like one other thing that Ratz said. "Still," he admits, "We can't plug all the descriptors into a computer and get a divine printout."[18]

Is there a type of pastor who "wears well" and stays longer? Maybe, but knowing this is not a just cause for staying or moving. The purpose of a pastor's self-awareness is to help develop counter-strengths and reactions that will enhance the chances of his staying longer. For further study about personality types and longevity, refer to the *Myers-Briggs Type Indicator* in Appendix C. You may find it helpful in increasing your own self-awareness.

Pastors who use self-understanding to manage their ministries have a greater chance of staying longer. They know their tendencies, their reaction to conflict and challenge and their willingness to grow and change with their people. Knowing these things does not excuse short-term pastorates; instead, it helps a pastor deal with the weaknesses and tendencies that often lead to the earlier-than-should-be termination of ministry.

Endnotes

1. Roy Oswald, *The Pastor as Newcomer* (Washington, DC: Alban Institute, 1977), Preface.
2. Lyle Schaller, *Survival Tactics in the Parish* (Nashville: Abingdon, 1977), p. 22.
3. Ibid.
4. Robert Schuller, *Your Church Has Real Possibilities* (Glendale, CA: Regal, 1974), p. 73.
5. G. Lloyd Rediger, *Coping with Clergy Burnout* (Valley Forge, PA: Judson Press, 1982), p. 41.

6. Allen Nauss, "The Relation of Pastoral Mobility to Effectiveness," *Review of Religious Research*, Winter 1974, p. 96.
7. John C. Fletcher, *Religious Authenticity in Clergy* (Washington, DC: Alban Institute, 1975), p. 3.
8. Larry Osborne, *The Unity Factor* (Waco, TX: Word, 1989), p. 63.
9. Lyle Schaller, *Reflections of a Contrarian* (Nashville: Abingdon, 1989), p. 182.
10. Gerard Gillaspie, *The Restless Pastor* (Chicago: Moody, 1974), p. 22.
11. Carl George and Robert Logan, *Leading and Managing Your Church* (Old Tappan, NJ: Revell, 1987), p. 154.
12. Roy Oswald et al., *New Visions for the Long Pastorate* (Washington, DC: Alban Institute, 1983), p. 60.
13. Gillaspie, *The Restless Pastor*, p. 14.
14. Oswald et al., *New Visions*, p. 60.
15. *Ministry Currents*, Barna Research Group, 1992, pp. 4–5.
16. Edward Dobson, Speed Leas and Marshall Shelley, *Mastering Conflict and Controversy* (Waco, TX: Word, 1992), p. 114.
17. Ronald Wimberly, "Mobility in Ministerial Career Patterns," *Journal for the Scientific Study of Religion*, Vol. 10, 1971, pp. 249–253.
18. Paul Robbins, *When It's Time To Move* (Waco, TX: Word, 1985), p. 18.

• CHAPTER EIGHT •

MORE OBSTACLES

Pastor Ray (whom we met in chapter seven) stuck it out, through the time of opposition, through some of the obstacles to longevity, through his desire to quit. By the fifth year of his ministry, the opposition began melting away. His own spirit of confidence returned, and with it a time of achievement, maintenance and growth for the church.

As he approached 40, Ray was finally considered by the church people to be "their" pastor. The success he was experiencing in the church gave him a personally renewed perspective for ministry. His handling of the church difficulties developed in him new skills in handling problems. His acceptance by the church gave him a newer and larger vision for his ministry as well as a desire for his people to grow in holiness. It was another great day for pastoring.

In the sixth year of his ministry numerical church growth returned. A second morning service was added. New people were attracted to the church, including some quality leadership people. Attempts at evangelism were beginning to bear fruit in conversion growth. The church's ministry to youth was strengthened, its emphasis on missions was improved, and giving was up. Things couldn't have been better.

But then came a new set of problems. Beginning in his seventh year of ministry, Ray once again hit some barriers to continued ministry. While the church facilities were being enlarged, growth brought with it growing pains. There were occasional doctrinal disputes over such things as the charismatic gifts and the verbal inspiration of the Scriptures that needed to be addressed. These differences always seemed to take more effort and time than Ray thought they should.

With all of the church growth, activity and time demands, the lay leadership began to tire. The time spent on managing the more than 60 church employees drained volunteer and paid staff. The addition of a third morning service only added to the burden and stress of ministry. In the midst of all this growth and conflict, Ray wanted to quit—again.

Obstacles to pastoral longevity are no respecter of pastors, or churches, or denominations, or educational institutions. As we have already noted, a lack of awareness of the issues related to longevity, failure to plan for personal growth and lack of self-awareness are major obstacles to longevity. But there are four more obstacles we need to talk about. While two of the first three centered on the pastor, these last four also involve local churches and denominational leaders.

OBSTACLE #4: *Mismanagement of Conflict*

One of the most common reasons pastors leave churches is because of a *mismanagement of conflict*, whether between laypeople or between the church and the pastor. Rather than stay and work through the conflict, the pastor "senses the call of God" and moves to another church.

Conflict management is a key to longevity. "Where attention is paid to conflict management," writes William Hobgood, "general congregational life will be healthier. Good pastoral skills paired with good conflict management is the best key to health in the long pastorate." This is one area of church life and ministry where the "gap" we talked about in chapter three can be seen very clearly. When good conflict skills do not grow with pastoral skills, pastoral care can still continue but the church will be less able to deal with its differences. Hobgood's prognosis? "Only disease can result from this."[1]

Most long-tenured pastors studied by the Alban Institute exhibited growth in their ability to manage conflict. They had learned the relationship between good conflict management (which includes the *acknowledgement* of conflict) and healthy church life. They had also found that a longer pastorate made conflict resolution easier, because the pastor had deeper, more trusting relationships with the people. These long-term pastors had learned that managing conflict, while less appetizing than managing organizational life, was crucial to staying longer.[2]

It is human nature for sinful people to have conflicts; in any group of people it is unavoidable. Even the two opposite roles of a pastor as nurturing shepherd and prodding change-agent inevitably create some discomfort and conflict. How that conflict is handled or mishandled is vital to the future of the ministry of the pastor in that church.

The greatest danger in handling church conflict is the absence of communication between pastor and people. In congregations where conflict is avoided or buried, people stop talking to one another except in the most polite or cautious terms. When tensions are avoided and conflict is suppressed, the air gets stale and boring. And so can the ministry.

Pastors can sometimes overreact to conflict, sending out resumes at the first hint of trouble. "A lot of times something happens in a church that involves maybe five people, and the pastor assumes the whole congregation is against him, so he takes off," long-tenured pastor Wendell Boyer from Beloit, Wisconsin, remarked. "A conflict with even ten out of a hundred is not impossible to overcome. In the next church there might be twenty. You don't help anything by moving in such cases; instead, you must get on your face before God and work through the problem. You talk with the persons involved, pray with them, reconcile if possible, and keep ministering regardless."[3]

There are also the "inner conflicts" that tempt a pastor to leave. In his personal testimony, "Why I Have Stayed," Lynn Anderson talks about the times in a pastor's ministry when it is seldom good to move. It is seldom good to move, he says, when you are frustrated that church growth has plateaued. There is nothing like a plateaued church to create tension inside a pastor. This is not the time to move.

It is seldom good to move, according to Anderson, when a problem person is making you miserable. You will never find a church that does not have a least one resident "pain in the neck." And, finally, Anderson says it is seldom good to move when more money is offered elsewhere. The need and desire for a larger salary is one of the pressure points in a pastor's relationship to his own church. But this is no reason to end a pastorate.[4]

If a pastor can manage to stay through these inner and outer conflicts, the lessons he learns will help him handle the next conflict—and the next. In the process, he will be learning how to stay longer.

Sometimes a pastor sets himself up for conflict that shortens his ministry. If a pastor comes to a congregation all ready to change things rapidly, not taking into consideration the traditions of that congregation, he has more than likely set the stage for an early departure. "The testimony of most long-tenured pastorates is that things do not get quickly turned over in the early years of the pastorate."[5] One long-tenured pastor was asked why he had had to stay 20 years at his church before renewal took place. He answered, "I had to stay long enough to get rid of everyone who didn't want renewal."

To stay longer, pastors and churches need to learn how to manage conflict. They need to understand the dynamics of change. The pastor must learn the skills needed by an effective change agent. Nauss and Coiner encountered some of the frustration and bitterness felt by pastors who had moved because of conflict. In their study, they discovered that sometimes the church's desire for the status quo was as much a reaction to the inappropriate methods of initiating change attempted by the pastor as it was from their comfort with the way things were.

After three years of successful ministry, Pastor Jenkins began to notice signs of congregational discontent.

"When [the pastors] pushed for change and parishioners resisted, [the pastors] may have yielded to aggressive action, frustration, or self-pity."[6]

While the pastor may need to change how he handles conflict if he wants to stay longer, churches also need to take a look at how they contribute to the problem. Churches sometimes change pastors just to avoid having to get involved in active ministry. Rather than make the changes necessary to make the church more effective, these churches shift their energies to the removal of their present pastor, the search for a new one, the installation process and finally to the manipulating of the new pastor.[7]

In such situations, when a pastor chooses to dig in for a hard fight to shake people out of their complacency, conflict management skills will be vital to his ministry and the long-term health of the church. "If a church has perpetually solved its problem by getting rid of leadership, its welfare will not be served by pushing yet another pastor out," Roy Oswald argues. "That just repeats the negative cycle. Sometimes clergy need to hang in there with the support of their denomination."[8]

Did you notice Oswald's last sentence? "Sometimes clergy need to hang in there *with the support of their denomination.*" Denominational leaders need to accept their responsibility in conflict mismanagement, too. Many of these leaders are former pastors, and if they did not manage conflict well in their own pastorates, how can they be expected to do any differently as overseers of pastors and churches? When denominational leaders cannot effectively manage conflict, short-term pastorates increase.

When I asked pastors and laypeople the question, "What do you think contributes to short-term pastorates?" some of their answers pointed to the way conflict is handled on the district level:

"The district superintendent is too quick to side with the church rather than with the pastor, [instead of] being a neutral reconciler in the situation."

"The district superintendent can't handle conflict at the church level. He tends to pull a man too early from the church."

"The district superintendent suggests for men to move in the midst of the struggle."

In my own study, I noticed a marked improvement in one denomination's district longevity statistics during a particular period of time. When I looked into the reasons why, I found that during this period of time, a new district superintendent had been elected. This district leader brought with him a fresh and effective approach to handling church conflicts. When he applied his conflict management skills at the district level, the average length of pastorates in the district went up.

Mismanagement of conflict more often than not leads to a shortened ministry. Everyone has a share in this obstacle. No one can point the finger at anyone else and say, "It's their fault."

OBSTACLE #5: *Inadequate Pastor/Parish Relationship*

The fifth obstacle of an *inadequate pastor/parish relationship* is often the real root cause of conflict in the church. But the problems between a pastor and his people invlove more than just the way they handle conflict.

In his little book with the attention-grabbing title, *Potshots at the Preacher*, James Sparks presents John Fletcher's four stages in the growth of the relationship between pastor and people. Each stage has its "crisis" which must be resolved if they are to continue successfully working together.

After the "honeymoon"—during which the pastor is formally

called, shipped and installed—comes stage one. In stage one, the personal authenticity of the pastor and the people is tested. The pastor asks himself, "Is there enough personal reality in the core group of leaders to invite them into a deeper relationship with me?" And the leaders ask themselves, "Is there enough personal reality in the pastor to enter into a deeper relationship with him?" And both sides ask, "Can issues like power, authority and purpose be successfully negotiated between us?" If these questions about the pastor/people relationship are not answered satisfactorily, the church faces the crisis of "counterdependency." Can the pastor and people accept each other or will they begin avoiding each other?

Stage two in the relationship tests the professional authenticity of the pastor. The people ask, "Is there harmony between what the pastor says and what he does?" And the pastor asks, "Is there enough potential in this congregation to make it worth my while to stay?" The pastor is tempted at this stage to try and prove his worth to his congregation and the congregation is tempted to ask the pastor to be their savior/problem-solver. This is the crisis of "interdependency," in which both the pastor and congregation decide whether or not they will rely on their own efforts or depend on God for whatever happens.

Stage three in the pastor/people relationship tests particular authenticity. The congregation begins to realize that they have something to contribute to ministry and they ask, "What particular gifts do I have to offer in ministry?" At the same time, the pastor has worked through his need to be able to do everything, and he begins to ask, "How will the gifts we have as a pastor and congregation be shared in ministry and mission?" The crisis to be met and conquered in this stage is the tendency for a church to become "overdependent" on the pastor rather than recognizing his specific gifts and sharing the ministry responsibilities together.

As each of these stages is successfully encountered, the relationship between the pastor and the people deepens. They get to know each other better. Together they sidestep the pitfalls of avoidance, unreal expectations and one-man ministry. If the pastor and the people have met and answered the challenge of these three stages, they will find themselves enjoying stage four: the realization of a maturing Christian community on its own inward and outward journey.[9]

This outline of a pastor's relationship with his people is helpful for at least two reasons. First, it tells us that the pastor/people relationship is a process. Second, it shows us how important it is for a pastor and a congregation to be talking to each other; frozen communication between pastor and people sets the stage for a one-act play rather than a long-term production.

One of the concerns that a pastor and his people need to discuss—and one that can seriously strain their relationship—is the amount of active care that is shown for the pastor and his family. William Hobgood reminds us that care is not a one-way street. "Care in relationships that have lasted for a number of years will certainly become empty if it is only the pastor who has cared actively." He notes that it is crucial for the congregation to care for the pastor. "It goes without saying," he continues, "that anger, then depression, then great loneliness can be the deadly results of a lack of care by the people of the congregational community. . . . There is nothing that will bring about de-energization and lack of enthusiasm . . . more rapidly than when my family is troubled. Mutual ministry calls for the congregation to care for the pastor and family."[10]

Remember the "gap theory" in chapter three? Part of the gap that appears between a pastor and his people develops when neither the pastor nor the people give each other effective feedback. The pastor is reluctant to tell the congregation or the church board how he feels about the ministry, his living arrangements or the church's expectations of him. At the same time, the church is afraid to give the pastor the feedback he needs to make his ministry more effective. Often this kind of feedback doesn't occur until the pastor has already resigned. By that time, it is too late to do anything about it—the feedback is more a venting of frustration.

One of the most effective deterrents to ministerial deterioration is the development of a pastoral support system. G. Lloyd Rediger says that such a "sustaining support system" would include the pastor's friends and family.[11] But it needs to include more. Clergy in need of support suffer too long before their fatigue and frustration are recognized either by those closest to them or by the church. A congregational support system that gives both encouragement and feedback can help keep a man fresh and ready to stay longer.

Too many pastors lack this kind of support and feedback system. Hobgood comments out of his own research that "the most significant pitfall in the long pastorate is the absence of clear feedback between the pastor and laity."[12]

A pastor needs a place where he can talk to his church leadership about his ministry concerns. One of those concerns is his compensation package. More than 15 years ago Bonnie Ramsey, in an article with the interesting title, "Christian Workers Are Programmed for Poverty," expressed her concern over the number of short pastorates. She quoted Warren Wiersbe who said, "We are suffering today from the tragic consequences of short pastorates. Local churches too often remain small and weak because they lack long-term care of a concerned shepherd who will 'stay by the stuff.'" Ramsey went on to link low salaries to the problem of pastors changing churches frequently. Either the low compensation creates stress that causes other problems in his ministry, or the pastor is offered another ministry situation with a better salary package for his family.[13]

If pastors and churches felt freer to talk about such things as compensation, ministry strategy and personal concerns, maybe pastors would stay longer. Instead, the lack of pastor-to-people communication creates tensions and misunderstandings that eventually lead to a shortened ministry.

Before you have a chance to think otherwise, let me make it clear that the blame for an inadequate pastor/parish relationship cannot be placed on the pastor alone. Churches need to assume more responsibility. In an Alban Institute study of the feedback between pastors and laity, it was found that 51 percent of the laity placed the blame for inadequate pastor/people relationship on the laity. Only 24 percent said the fault was the pastor's.[14] Lay people acknowledge the problem. Now they must be willing to do something about it. They must realize that if they want to have pastors stay longer, they need to invest something besides moving costs into the care and "feedbacking" of their pastor.

It seems, though, that some churches are better at fostering poor relationships with their pastors. Roy Oswald mentioned to me in a personal conversation that many smaller churches function as "tribes." These churches have their own hierarchy. The pastor is treated as an invited guest, a holy one at that, but he is never allowed to be in control. When the pastor begins to get too settled and rooted, these people in control of the tribe begin to get uneasy. It is only a matter of time until the pastor is nudged out. This cycle is repeated with pastor after pastor. There is a wall built between the pastor and the church.

Another dynamic working against a good pastor/church relationship is the confused expectations people in the church have about the pastor's role and function. In his work with pastors and churches, John Davis, director of a career development center in Minnesota, noticed that this confusion often causes unnecessary and avoidable tensions between a pastor and his church members. When a church does not know, or does not agree on what their pastor should be, or should be doing, a pastor will easily tire of trying to meet the congregation's undefined expectations. Uncertainty and indefinite expectations do not create a healthy environment for any pastor who wishes to develop a long-term ministry.

A church needs to take more of the responsibility for creating an environment conducive to longevity. The impression often is that a church stands back and watches its pastors come and go with a sense of helplessness and wonder. By watching and doing nothing to work for a better pastor/people relationship, a church has encouraged a shorter pastorate, whether it intended to or not.

On the other hand, "congregations which foster healthy long-tenured pastorates . . . accept clergy as human, allow room for failure, have a willingness to work with the clergy on common goals, use problem solving rather than blame in dealing with troublesome issues and are open to new input, ideas, and members."[15]

It takes two sides to work at longevity—the pastor and the church. As Oswald notes, "When one gives much more than the other, then there is burnout." That results in more short-term ministries.

OBSTACLE #6: *Faulty Early Patterns*

You may have noticed that we are not discussing these obstacles in any particular order. If we were, the obstacle of *faulty early patterns* would have to be at least number one or number two, for it can develop rather early in a pastor's experience.

We have already said that a pastor's wrong assumptions about longevity affect his own longevity pattern. To some degree, those false assumptions began very early, with a lack of awareness fostered by the educational institution he attended. What might be harder to recognize is what happens next in the making of a pastor and how it encourages these false assumptions about longevity.

Listen to what several pastors said as they reflected on their early years of ministry:

> "My first church was short-term [three years] by the design of the district. . . . This helped to set the tone and mind of short-term pastorates for the future."
> "My first pastorate could have been longer and it would have been good for me for future patterns."
> "My whole attitude [toward longer pastorates] would have changed had I been in my first church longer. I developed a mind-set of short-term."

Did you catch it? Did you hear what happens? A pastor's initial ministries set the tone for much of the rest of his career. If his first couple of pastorates are short, the chances are very great that he will have a career of short pastorates.

When Burdette Palmberg, pastor of a church in Mercer Island, Washington neared graduation, his casual curiosity turned into a preoccupation with finding a church. As he considered his own entrance into the professional ministry he kept thinking about one statistic: the average length of a pastor's first pastorate. It was just over two years![16] If these are the early patterns of the average first-time pastor, is it any wonder that future pastorates won't be much longer?

And the opposite is also true. Early experiences with a long-term ministry encourages subsequent long-term pastorates. One long-term pastor commented to me, "At least in my case, it seems that long-term pastorates breed long-term pastorates."

In Lyle Schaller's imaginary small group of pastors, Marty Lusik speaks of her husband Dick and his pattern of changing pastorates:

> "It has suddenly occurred to me that part of our problem is that Dick wrote a two-chapter book as a curate after graduation from seminary. Next he wrote a two-chapter volume as rector at Calvary, and now we are at the end of the second chapter at Trinity." As she spoke, she turned toward her husband and asked, "Maybe, Dick, we need to learn now to write a third chapter rather than start a new volume after chapter two?"[17]

Dick and Marty were stuck in a pattern of short pastorates that had its roots in the very first years of their ministry career. Marty recognized that since they had known nothing else, a conscious choice must be made to change the pattern.

The trouble is that a pastor's first pastorate is commonly assumed to be an "apprenticeship" that lasts long enough for him to get his feet wet and then move to another, more established work. "Typically this [first pastorate] is a two-to-four year pastorate, and many times it is an unofficial apprenticeship for the new minister," writes Schaller.[18] A pastor's first pastorate has also been labeled as a time of "career establishment," lasting no more than three to five years. It serves mainly to help the young pastor adjust to the professional ministry.[19]

Whatever it is called, these early years of ministry set patterns for a lifetime of ministry in many areas. A study by two seminary professors bears this out. They contend that the "first experience as a parish pastor may be more influential than seminary training in shaping the role and self-imposed expectations of the clergy."[20]

And one of those patterns is an idea and a feel for how long a pastorate should be. How the young minister responds the first time he encounters some of the obstacles to longevity can affect the rest of his life. The lessons a young minister learns by staying longer in his first pastorate are invaluable for his future pastorates.

Normally, however, a pastor takes his first church unaware of the obstacles to staying longer. For instance, Gillaspie says that the third year of a man's first ministry is undoubtedly the most difficult. By that time, the "first flush of enthusiasm has subsided and the novelty has worn off." He says that the true test of a man's ministry is whether or not he can survive that third year, the time just after the initial excitement is gone and just before any of the hoped-for results begin to materialize. "Anyone can succeed one year, most two years, but only the genuine article can survive the third year. Pass that safely and find the fourth better and the fifth better still."[21] A young pastor who hits that "third-year wall" without realizing the importance of staying through it, will do what he has seen others do. He will leave too soon. He will also have taken his first step toward a pattern of short-term ministries.

The younger the first-time pastor is, the greater the tendency to see a shorter pastorate as the norm. "The twenty-six-year-old pastor often sees a four-year pastorate as the norm while the fifty-five-year-old minister may remark, 'Why, it takes at least three or four years to know the people and to be able to set your priorities. Anything less than seven years is really too short for a pastorate nowadays.' "[22]

In their study of first parish pastors, Nauss and Coiner attempted to identify a minimum time period for a worthwhile stay by a minister in his first parish. They concluded that a man should stay in his first church at least three-and-one-half years to do the church any good.[23] Another professor said, "Stay three years and you can stay a lifetime." Others have encouraged men to stay in their first pastorate at least five, six or eight years.[24]

Lyle Schaller suggests that the length of a pastor's first pastorate in a rural congregation (often a man's first stop on the ecclesiastical yellow brick road) depends on the man's background and long-term goals. If, for instance, the young pastor is from a large suburban church with an urban or suburban background, Schaller says that he will learn all he'll ever need to know about rural America and the small church in four years. By the middle of the fourth year, the man will have passed the peak of his learning curve for that type of experience and he should think about moving on to someplace new and more challenging. On the other hand, if the young man intends to make rural ministry his career, then he needs to stay longer. He will need about five years to get to know the people in sufficient depth to understand them. By the sixth or seventh year he may have enough trust to introduce some new ideas to improve and expand ministry. After reaching the peak of the learning curve at about year five, if a young pastor stays another six or seven years to build on that foundation, Schaller says that he should be able to make a lasting difference in the lives of those people and in the ministry and outreach of that congregation.[25]

I personally believe a man should stay longer than the average if he wants to do not only the church any good, but himself any good. I say this because of something else that Nauss and Coiner discovered. They found that both the "stayers" and "movers" used the same reason for staying or leaving their first church. Both were responding to a new challenge. The "movers" were responding to a new challenge somewhere else while the "stayers" saw the challenge in their present church.[26] To twist a phrase, "the challenge is in the eye of the beholder."

What does this mean for a young pastor's future longevity? As he anticipates a lifetime of ministry, he will more than likely start on the low ladder rung of ministry placement, advancing to higher levels of increased responsibility over the years. The usual pattern is to stay on each "rung" only long enough to gain sufficient experience to be promoted to the next rung. Each new rung, as you might expect, comes complete with new challenges.

Consequently, if a pastor is always attracted to new challenges outside his church, in another pastorate, he won't be staying very long in any one place. But if a pastor can, beginning with his first church, start to see the challenges in his present ministry, he will be developing an important dynamic that will allow him to write chapter after chapter in one place. This is one reason why a man's first pattern in longevity is more important than it might seem.

After conducting my own interviews with pastors and laypeople, the importance of early patterns was clear. It seems that the pastor's early experience will set the stage for duplication later, whether the pattern being repeated is that of a long-term or short-term ministry. Just as churches tend to repeat previous patterns, so do pastors. I noticed that churches specifically looking for a man to stay longer as their pastor will look for a man who has already done it somewhere else. In the same way, pastors who start with shorter pastorates will have a harder time breaking that faulty early pattern unless they choose to do so.

Just how important early patterns are can be seen in one related study done on "Persistence in Seminary and Ministry" by Sue Cardwell, professor at Christian Theological Seminary in Indianapolis, Indiana. She commented on the importance of a pastor having models of longevity in his own life, beginning with the his own home church's experience with longer pastorates. "The greater the number of ministers who had served a person's home church while [he was] growing up, the more likely he was not to persist in ministry."[27] While "persistence in ministry" is not exactly the same thing as pastoral longevity, the dynamics are similar enough for us to say that a person's early example and experience with longevity cannot help but affect one's own pattern of longevity.

Early patterns are crucial. The challenges and conflicts of those first years will be repeated in future ministries. If a pastor learns to deal with the conflicts and failures correctly in his first church, he will be more likely to experience a longer pastorate and to experience it sooner. Unfortunately, many men deal with conflicts, failures and disappointments by leaving that first church. The only "experience" they have gained is how to run from conflicts, failure and disappointment. But if a young pastor can learn in that first church to dream visions and set goals that will last beyond two to three years, and then work to make them happen, he will probably stay longer in his first church, and even longer in his next one.

OBSTACLE #7: Unsatisfactory Pastoral Transitions

For years we have suspected that the American system of mate selection has something to do with the rise in the divorce rate. In countries where parents select their child's future spouse, marriage is initially more a contract of commitment than a romance. But in America, marriages are based more on romance than commitment. So when the romance wears off, the marriage partners take off. The American system for mate selection seems to be faulty. We call the American system for mate selection dating. Driven by passion, romance and first impression, it sets couples up for disillusionment and divorce.

The same can be said for the pastoral selection process. Driven by first impressions, lofty expectations and weekend romances, churches and pastors select each other for better or worse—until the honeymoon is over and the romance wears off after a couple of years. And it is the ecclesiastical "dating" system that is partly to blame for pastorates that end too soon. Obstacle #7 we can call *unsatisfactory pastoral transitions*.

How a district superintendent, a local church pastoral search committee and a pastoral candidate choose which church will get which pastor is sometimes a mystery. Laypeople don't

"Why can't he just read his resignation like other pastors do?"

Copyright 1979 Larry Thomas. Used by permission.

understand it. Denominational leadership wants to understand it. And pastoral candidates think they understand it. But more often than it should, what started out as a clergy-parish romance ends in a disappointing mismatch, painful disillusionment and sooner-than-necessary departure.

And it all begins with that notorious "candidating weekend." Gillaspie writes, "Many new church-pastor relationships get off to an unhealthy start simply because there was not sufficient investigation. The candidating encounter was not well-planned, not thorough, and not of sufficient length."[28]

Who is to blame? Can we say the "system" and leave it at that? Not quite. Somebody decides the system, somebody runs the system, somebody participates in the system.

When I asked pastors and laypeople about the pastoral selection process, they knew it needed improving.

> "The district superintendent doesn't take care in placing men in the district."
> "The candidating system is a horrible lottery system for pastors and churches."
> "The pastor is often misrepresented to the church."

We may never change the American mate selection process (I know, I tried to contract my daughters for marriage, but they didn't quite like the idea!). And we may not be able to change our particular system of pastoral selection, but we can improve it. District superintendents can improve it, churches can improve it, pastoral candidates can improve it.

Beyond the candidating process, there is another side to pastoral transitions that leads to shorter-than-necessary pastorates. The exit that a pastor makes from his previous church is just as important as his placement into a new church. The word transitions includes both pastoral *selection* and pastoral *ejection!*

When a pastor leaves a church, all too often he moves on with unresolved feelings that will affect his next ministry. He carries with him patterns that will handicap his desire to stay longer at the next place. If those feelings and patterns are not acknowledged and dealt with as part of his transition, a pastor between churches is setting himself up for another early departure. Just as there is "marriage on the rebound," so there is pastoral selection on the rebound. Both pastors and churches do it.

Pastors and churches need to learn how to select each other better. Roy Oswald notes that "we have not discovered any training taking place . . . that equips clergy to deal with transitions."[29] We can safely add that neither has there been much attention paid to helping churches and denominational leadership improve the system of pastoral transitions.

Greater care for pastors in transition and churches in transition is needed. Denominational leadership is in a position to provide that care. The pastoral selection process must do more than just put a warm body in a pulpit vacancy. The process must pay attention to the assistance of pastors and churches in transition. It must create a better chance for the kind of commitment from each other that pastors and churches are hoping will become a reality. Too many "blind dates" and "rebound relationships" have resulted in too-short pastorates.

Ray stayed. In spite of the problems, pressures and desire to quit, he didn't move. He stayed for another 13 years! And was he ever glad he did. If he hadn't, he would have missed the church-wide revival that lasted for several years. He would have missed a wider ministry to the larger body of Christ. He would have missed the development of a strong home base of prayer support and the special times of congregational "waiting on God."

Instead of giving in to his inclination to quit, Ray Ortlund stayed longer where he was. Then he wrote a book to share with us his life message: *You Don't Have to Quit.* At the very beginning he says, "Everywhere jobs are quit too soon, schooling is cut too soon, marriages are severed too soon, friendships are broken too soon—switching and dropping out have become epidemic. It's time to cry, 'Hold it!' "[30]

Endnotes

1. William Hobgood, "The Long-Tenured Pastorate: A Study of Ways to Build Trust," Unpublished Thesis, Lancaster (PA) Seminary, 1982, pp. 56–57.
2. Roy Oswald et al., *New Visions for the Long Pastorate* (Washington, DC: Alban Institute, 1983), p. 76.
3. "Shepherds Who Have Stayed," *Leadership*, p. 142.
4. Lynn Anderson, "Why I Have Stayed," *Leadership*, Summer 1986, pp. 79–80.
5. Hobgood, "The Long-Tenured Pastorate," p. 71.
6. Allen Nauss and Harry Coiner, "The First Parish: Stayers and Movers," *Review of Religious Research*, Winter 1971, p. 100.
7. *Ministry Trends*, Barna Research Group, p. 6.
8. Roy Oswald, "The Pastor's Passages," *Leadership*, Fall 1983, p. 17.
9. James Sparks, *Potshots at the Preacher* (Nashville: Abingdon, 1977), pp. 98–100.
10. Hobgood, "The Long-Tenured Pastorate," p. 64–65
11. G. Lloyd Rediger, *Coping with Clergy Burnout* (Valley Forge, PA: Judson, 1982), pp. 13–14.
12. Hobgood, "The Long-Tenured Pastorate," p. 57
13. Bonnie Ramsey, "Christian Workers Are Programmed for Poverty," *Moody*, June 1976, p. 80–81.
14. Roy Oswald et al., *New Visions for the Long Pastorate*, p. 64.
15. Ibid. p. 41.
16. Burdette Palmberg, "The Breaking of a Minister," *Leadership*, Summer 1986, p. 60.
17. Lyle Schaller, *Survival Tactics in the Parish* (Nashville: Abingdon, 1977), p. 22.

18. Ibid. p. 27.
19. Charles Stewart, *Person and Profession* (Nashville: Abingdon, 1974), pp. 27–28.
20. Lyle Schaller, *Reflections of a Contrarian* (Nashville: Abingdon, 1989), p. 180.
21. Gerald Gillaspie, *The Restless Pastor* (Chicago: Moody, 1974), p. 21.
22. Lyle Schaller, *The Middle-Sized Church* (Nashville: Abingdon, 1985), p. 124.
23. Nauss and Coiner, "The First Parish," p. 95.
24. Gillaspie, *The Restless Pastor,* p. 21.
25. Schaller, *Contrarian,* p. 124–125.
26. Nauss and Coiner, "The First Parish," p. 99.
27. Caldwell, Sue, and Richard Hunt, "Persistence in Seminary and Ministry," *Journal of Pastoral Psychology,* Winter 1979, pp. 119–131.
28. Gillaspie, *The Restless Pastor,* p. 12.
29. Roy Oswald, *The Pastor as Newcomer* (Washington, DC: Alban Institute, 1977), p. 3.
30. Anne and Ray Ortlund, *You Don't Have to Quit* (Nashville: Nelson, 1986), front cover.

CHAPTER NINE

THE STRATEGIES

Pastor Paul Andrews was in trouble. After ten years of ministry at Calvary Chapel, people were starting to talk. And he was starting to agree with them. His preaching wasn't what it should be. The ministry was drying up. He felt like he was drifting.

About that time, Paul ran into his old seminary professor, Dr. Vickerson. As Paul shared his concerns, his old mentor once again took him under his wing. They began spending some time together, talking about how to rejuvenate his ministry so he could stay longer.

During one visit, as they were returning to Dr. Vickerson's apartment with his favorite food, pizza, Dr. Vickerson commented to Paul, "A few years out of seminary and that reservoir runs dry, usually about the same time the enthusiasm for the ministry starts to wane. It's a deadly combination, leaving the preacher with little left to say and even less desire to say it. So he starts to struggle with whether or not it's time to leave."

The elevator door opened and the two men stepped out into the hallway. As Dr. Vickerson reached for his keys he concluded. "Then guess what happens, Paul?"

"The minister accepts a call to another congregation," Paul offered.

"Right," responded Dr. V. "And when he gets to the new church he's enthusiastic and they're enthusiastic. His preaching is fresh and new to them, not like the preacher that has just left. But what they don't know is that the new minister is not saying anything new and fresh at all; he's merely repeating himself from his prior ministry."

"So for awhile the ministry is new and fun again, then the same pattern repeats itself," Paul mused. "That's the very reason I've hesitated in moving for so long. I keep thinking that the problems will pack up and move with me."

"It will, Paul, it will," countered the old professor. "That's why you must break the vicious cycle here and now, right where you are. Not just for your sake, but for the people, too, and especially for the glory of God!"

"For too long the church has been plagued with ministers who repeat their three-year ministries six times in six different churches. Instead of eighteen years of experience in the ministry, they really only have three years repeated six times. It's a terrible problem that has greatly harmed the cause of Christ in the world. It has to be stopped, Paul. In your life it has to be stopped."[1]

Author Bruce Mawhinney's fictional Dr. Vickerson is right. The pattern of short pastorates needs to be stopped. Pastors need to start taking seriously the vow of stability. Churches need to help their pastors stay longer. But how? What can be done to overcome the obstacles to longevity?

In this chapter, I would like to offer some helpful suggestions and point to some available resources in dealing with the issue of longevity. Although there is no guaranteed solution to the problem, I believe that these suggestions and resources can help create a better environment in which denominational leadership, local churches and pastors can see an increase in the length of pastoral ministries. I would encourage you to find additional resources that you can use to implement these strategies.

Let's briefly review the seven obstacles to longevity we have identified:

1. lack of awareness
2. lack of personal growth
3. lack of self-understanding
4. mismanagement of conflict
5. inadequate pastor/people relationship
6. faulty early patterns
7. unsatisfactory pastoral transitions

Now let's begin the job of working to manage these obstacles. For each obstacle, there is a strategy to begin the successful management of each barrier.

STRATEGY #1: *Increase Awareness*

In dealing with the obstacle, lack of awareness, strategy #1 sounds simple. And it can be. We have noted that all four members of the longevity team lack awareness—educational institutions, denominational leadership, pastors and churches. Each can do something to become more acquainted with the challenges and concerns of pastoral longevity.

Suggestions for Educational Institutions

First of all, I would suggest that schools hold at least one faculty brainstorming session to discuss and develop ideas of how to integrate the issues of longevity into the existing ministry classes.

Secondly, the curriculum for pastors-in-training should include a unit on the dynamics of longevity. Portions of this book could be used to heighten awareness of the advantages and disadvantages of short-term and long-term pastorates. Pastors and laypeople in healthy, longer pastorates could be invited to talk about the topic of longevity. Students could be assigned to observe and report on a particular pastor's long-term ministry. And issues which are addressed in other parts of the curriculum (such as personal relationships, self-understanding, conflict management and personal growth) could be related to the goal of pastoral longevity.

Suggestions for Pastors

Pastors should take responsibility for their own need to become more aware of the benefits and behaviors of longevity. I would encourage them to take some time to read several of the articles and books referred to in the bibliography (see entries 7, 17, 42, 47, 85). It wouldn't hurt for local church leaders to do the same. In fact, I would encourage pastors and church leaders to sit down for a couple of hours to talk openly to one another about the desirability of pastors staying longer, what it means and how it can be accomplished.

Suggestions for Churches

A church that finds itself between pastors should spend a month discussing this issue before they get involved in the pastoral search process. I would suggest that books or articles be selected for reading and discussion (see bibliography entries 42, 99). The time between pastors is a great opportunity for such a study, since no pastor would be threatened by the honest comments of laypeople. And the laypeople could express their opinions and desires without having a specific pastor in mind.

Suggestions for Denominational Leadership

Denominational leaders would also benefit from the insight and information gathered in this book and others about longevity. If national and regional church leaders are to be part of the solution to the challenge of pastors staying longer, they need to be more familiar with the subject.

The leadership can do more than simply educate itself about longevity—it can also encourage awareness by planning seminars and training on the topic. Regional leadership should introduce the subject of longevity to churches between pastors .

These suggestions are by no means comprehensive, but I hope they are a start toward increasing awareness about longevity.

STRATEGY #2: Plan for Personal Growth

In his 15th volume of *Journals and Letters*, John Wesley wrote, "I know that, were I myself to preach one whole year in one place, I should preach both myself and most of my congregation asleep."[2] While most pastors take a bit longer to preach their people asleep, the truth is, unless a pastor is developing his own skills and developing himself as a person, he will reach a point of crisis. Either he must grow or leave. In other words, for a pastor to stay longer, he needs to *plan for personal growth.*

The pastor's own style and pace of ministry may demand that he grow in order to stay longer. Pastors who try to do too much usually reach a burnout point—sometimes as early as three years into their ministry. To release themselves from the unbearable strain, the first solution they think of is to change churches. What would happen if, instead of taking their burnout pattern somewhere else, these pastors were to take some time to grow through this stage. They could learn to pace themselves, take care of themselves, keep themselves fresh and develop new skills for leadership and ministry. Both they and their churches would be better off—and they might stay together longer.

The nature of the work and the worker demands that a pastor plan for personal growth. "Vocational theorists acknowledge that persons become bored with their jobs over time, and that seven years is about the maximum length of time one can tolerate doing the same thing without some change in the role. Ministers are no exception to this rule."[3] This is not saying that a pastor must change *where* he works to avoid boredom, just that he should think about changing *within* his role. This kind

"My congregation took up an offering for my continuing education. Know of any conferences for $7.22?"

of change happens when a man is willing to grow, and when a church is willing to let him grow.

The passage of time is no guarantee that growth is happening; aging is not necessarily the same thing as growing. And a pastor must be responsible for his own personal and professional growth—no one can do it for him. Some pastors just don't know how to plan for their personal development. Others simply fail to look for mental, spiritual or physical stimulation to stay effective in ministry.

The number and variety of resources for a pastor's personal growth can seem overwhelming. I would like to suggest a simple outline as a "beginner's plan" for growth:

1. Take some time to become familiar with the issues of personal and professional growth. The bibliography contains several books which will introduce the professional minister to these issues (see entries 11, 59, 76). Talk to former professors or contemporary colleagues about the what, how, why, when and where of personal and professional development. Ask such questions as, "What are other pastors doing? How do I talk to my board about it? Why would I select certain growth opportunities rather than others? When is the best time? Where can I find new resources for personal development?"

2. Try to take advantage of a minimum of 50 hours of continuing education per year. While 50 hours is no "magic number," it is a common figure suggested as a goal for pastors who want to stay growing and keep their people from falling asleep on them!

3. Go beyond continuing education and work at developing a balanced approach to all of life's activities, including recreation, inner spiritual disciplines, family time and relationships with colleagues. Lack of mental stimulation is not the sole cause of burnout. It is a combination of factors, all pointing to a life out of balance. The older you get and the longer you are in the ministry, the greater the tendency to become brittle and narrow—and brittle, narrow pastors move a lot more often. Keeping variety and balance in your schedule will

postpone the onset of ministerial sclerosis.

4. Discuss with your church the possibility of pastoral sabbaticals. "It is ludicrous to believe," the Alban Institute researchers contend, "that year after year a pastor can be continually profound in weekly Sunday sermons without periodic opportunities to get away for an extended time."[4] They suggest a three-month sabbatical every few years. Such a plan may not be possible for every church, but the point is well taken. Churches need to recognize the value of pace and space in a pastor's life. And pastors need to be willing to admit that they can't go on "solar power" forever. They need time to regenerate so they don't degenerate.

Educational and denominational leaders are part of the strategy, too. Schools can lay an important foundation for a lifetime of learning. We are all familiar with the frequent articles written by ministers that say something about the "things they didn't teach you in school." What these articles are really saying is: schools may not teach us all we need to know, but they can show us *how to teach ourselves* what we need to know.

College and seminary training should include instruction on planning for personal growth throughout one's career, but especially during the early years of ministry. Remember how important those early patterns are!

Denominational leaders can help by educating local churches on the importance of their pastor's personal growth. They should also consider sponsoring some personal renewal opportunities for pastors.

John Wesley never had to stay in one place very long, but today's pastor does. To stay fresh in that one place, a pastor needs to plan for personal renewal. "To survive the long pastorate," Roy Oswald writes, "it is essential to take a long view of one's call and learn to feel at home with the changes of agendas, able to handle both success and failure. Although there may be peaks of good times, and valleys of bad, long-tenured pastors must learn to maintain energy and focus through them all."[5]

I will never forget what one lay leader said to me several years ago when I presented my plan for further schooling to my church board: "A growing pastor means a growing people." That's a great attitude and the right perspective. A church, its leadership and its pastor need to plan for personal growth in the life of the pastor, and provide the time and resources for that to happen.

STRATEGY #3: Deepen Self-Understanding

Pastor Larry felt trapped. He thought he had found a new church, but the search committee had called another candidate. While he didn't want to leave his present church just to be leaving, he also didn't want to continue in a ministry of keeping people happy and maintaining the status quo. His one option that had looked so promising—taking another church—had fallen through. Now he felt more discouraged than ever.

It was then that Larry began to learn something about himself. Instead of stewing in his frustration, he began to direct that energy toward something he wanted most of all. "I couldn't see clearly for a long while what my discouragement was coming from. But as I pinpointed it to my need for a new challenge, I thought, 'What could be a bigger challenge than trying to lead this congregation into the growth I can see for it?' I knew these people, and by now I'd built a level of trust with them. If anybody was going to do it, it would be me."[6]

When Larry was forced to take a personal inventory, he learned some new things about himself and his ministry. As a result, he ended up staying longer—much longer. This leads us to a third strategy to increase pastoral longevity: ***deepen self-un-***

derstanding. The better a pastor knows his strengths, his weaknesses, his style, his tendencies in conflict and his approach to adversity, the more prepared he will be to deal with the obstacles and challenges to staying longer.

Personality tests often help increase a person's self-understanding, and many times the results can be applied to the question of longevity. For instance, the Minnesota Multi-Phasic Inventory measures the "energy level" of an individual. This measurement can provide insight into a pastor's tendency to be actively mobile.

A healthy understanding of one's leadership style and the ability to be flexible as a leader is an important component for staying longer in one place of ministry. Norman Shawchuck's *Church Leadership Kit* (see bibliography) is a helpful tool for aiding a pastor in identifying his primary and backup style of leadership. It educates the pastor in other leadership styles available to him for different periods of his ministry, and also gives him the opportunity to "practice" styles of leadership that might be new for him. In addition, the kit is designed to offer laypeople the chance to give their pastor constructive feedback on his leadership style.

The Myers-Briggs Type Indicator is another tool for evaluating personality and its relationship to longevity. While we have yet to find an instrument which specifically identifies whether a pastor will stay short term or long term, the Myers-Briggs Type Indicator comes pretty close. A fuller explanation and application of Myers-Briggs is provided in Appendix C.

We must remember that the purpose for self-understanding is not to excuse our tendencies and weaknesses, but to discover what skills and strengths we need to develop to increase our chances of being able to maintain the vow of stability.

STRATEGY #4: Strengthen Conflict Management Skills

The new American definition of freedom is the freedom to be unencumbered. When problems arise, we think we ought to be free to move on—to a new city, a new job, a new marriage or a new church. Accordingly, our society has taken on the language of progress to talk about this moving around. We talk about "moving on," "moving beyond" and "how far we have come." We seem to have confused movement with progress.[7]

Sometimes we make the same false connection in ministry. When problems or conflicts arise in the pastorate, the greatest tendency is to move on. We somehow feel free to leave the conflict behind. And we call going to a new church "progress," when the real progress would have been to stay and learn how to work through the problem or conflict.

You may remember that obstacle #4 to pastoral longevity was the *mismanagement of conflict*. To deal with this obstacle, strategy #4 is to *strengthen conflict management skills*.

When a pastor doesn't effectively handle conflict in the church, the seeds of his departure are sown. But just as responsible is the local church that fails to properly handle conflict, or even tries to deny it. Such a church becomes a breeding ground for short-term pastorates. Also responsible are denominational leaders, when they fail to assist pastors and local churches in dealing with conflict. More often than is necessary, the pastor is removed before he or the church can learn how to handle conflict properly.

The first conflict between a pastor and his people brings disillusionment and questions. How they deal with the problem is all too often ill-informed, based on poor models, or simply a reaction to past experiences.

Our schools can be a part of strategy #4 by teaching future

pastors how to manage conflict *before* they encounter it. Educators can extend the school's teaching site beyond the classroom by providing in-service training in the area of conflict management for pastors and churches in the field.

In some situations, the pastor can teach his church to successfully manage conflict. In other cases, regional leadership is better able to offer help for pastors and local churches. However it is done, strengthening conflict management skills will be an important part of the strategy to increase pastoral longevity. The bibliography contains several books and resources on this critical topic (see entries 30, 31, 32, 40, 62, 72, 74, 79, 119).

STRATEGY #5: *Improve Pastor/Congregation Relations*

At the risk of stating the obvious, the relationship between a pastor and his people is crucial in any discussion of pastoral longevity. If the relationship is strained or broken, the chances of the pastor lasting much longer are slim. Strategy #5, then, is to *improve pastor/congregation relations.*

At the risk of once again stating the obvious, improving relations between the pastor and the people is easier said than done. It's like telling a child to love his or her brother or sister. You can speak it. You can hope it. But what can you do to make it actually happen?

Here is a practical, though not original, suggestion: develop a pastor/congregation relations committee. William Hobgood calls such a committee "the most important tool that the local congregation can use for pastor/parish health." This committee works with the pastor in helping him evaluate the church and his relationship to it, discusses with the pastor his terms and expectations of employment, and serves as a "think tank" for the changes the pastor may need to make in his own ministry style as the church develops. During times of possible tension between the pastor and the congregation, this committee would be ready to help the pastor deal with the questions and solutions.

Resistance to a pastor/congregation relations committee is surprisingly high in many churches. One way to alleviate some of the hesitation and apprehension, Hobgood suggests, is to start the committee at the beginning of a pastorate rather than in the middle of a man's ministry.[8]

A pastor/congregation relations committee meets the need for communication between the pastor and the people and also monitors how the people are taking care of their pastor. Lyle Schaller says that the focus of this committee is not on answering

"The trouble with preaching a really great sermon is that now I can't use it again till I get another church."

© 1988 Lee Johnson

the pastor's question, "Do you like me?" but on evaluating the ministry and performance of the pastor *and* the people.

Schaller also suggests that it is unwise for the committee to discuss such sensitive issues as the pastor's salary until it has practiced its relational skills, developed into a fairly close-knit group and is recognized as a regular standing committee of the church. Before it can deal with questions of the pastor's employment, this group must earn the respect of other church committees which may have formerly handled such items. The duties of this committee should at first be few, then increased year by year.

Though it may vary according to differences in church polity, Schaller suggests that the committee be appointed by the church board rather than elected by the membership, and consist of about seven members selected for three-year terms to promote continuity. During a pastoral vacancy, the committee should be dissolved and start up again no later than six months after the new pastor has arrived unless the new pastor objects to the existence of such a committee.

Schaller says the make-up of the committee should include a person who can function as an advocate for the pastor's wife, a person who can do the same thing on behalf of the pastor, someone who knows about the care of the parsonage, a member of the church board, a member of the finance committee, a member from the original pastoral search committee and a person-centered chairman.

The committee, according to Schaller, should have at least 10 meetings a year, with each regular meeting covering a different major topic, such as the pastor's wife and family, the congregation's expectations, the congregation's performance, the condition of the parsonage, the pastor's compensation, church staff, the pastor's plans and continuing education. Other duties of the committee could include responsibility for reception of new staff, staff birthdays, anniversaries, employment anniversaries and discussion about ministry offers from other churches looking for a pastor.[9]

Committee members should do some study on the pressures and problems of the ministry to help them understand their pastor better. Two books on this topic are Lucille Lavender's *They Cry Too!* and Edward Bratcher's *The Walk on the Water Syndrome* (see bibliography entries 29, 6).

There is always a lot of talk about the relationship between the pastor and the congregation, but usually very little action. Innovative approaches such as the pastor/congregation relations committee can improve the chances of pastors and churches staying together longer (see bibliography entry 116). "Sometimes the premature urge of the minister to look for greener pastures elsewhere or of laymen to seek new pastoral leadership can be responded to most creatively by their working together in a re-evaluation of the work of the parish, rather than looking for a new team or seeking a new manager."[10]

STRATEGY #6: Encourage Longer Early Pastorates

Low-commitment churches (where not much is expected of members or the ministry) produce low-commitment pastors, who end up serving three to four years and then move on.[11] And very often this pattern of low commitment and short-term pastorates begins early in a pastor's career, as early as his first pastorate. A faulty early pattern, though less obvious, is a very real obstacle to longevity. To help manage this obstacle, we need strategy #6—*encouraging longer early pastorates.*

Encouraging young pastors to stay longer in their early pastorates can begin while they are still in school, by increasing the students' awareness of longevity issues. Local churches can also help the young pastor by demonstrating an expectation and desire that he stay longer, by being patient with the mistakes of inexperience and by taking the time to set up an effective pastor/congregation relations committee. Denominational leaders may need to rethink their traditional expectations of a young pastor. Instead of acting like the first-time pastor will stay only two or three years, they should encourage him to stay five years or more, with a goal of staying longer and longer with each successive pastorate.

There are resources for the first-time pastor that can help him learn about and deal with the transition from school to pastorate (see bibliography entries 49, 50). A regional denominational leader may be able to organize a group study with several first-time pastors. As a young pastor realizes that many of his experiences and feelings are a "normal" part of adjustment, he will be less likely to blame the church, himself, or the ministry. And he will be less likely to leave the church too early.

As I visited with young men who were in their first church, and with laypeople from churches that historically have been first-church pastorates, I learned how important it is to encourage longer early pastorates. The young pastors had heard very little from the school or the denomination about staying longer in their first pastorate and developing a better sense of what it takes to be a pastor. I learned that churches, for the most part, had bought the ecclesiastical party line that men in their first church shouldn't stay very long. When I made the suggestion that first-time pastors should stay longer, the young pastors were intrigued by the idea and the laypeople expressed their desire to make it happen.

Together, we can increase pastoral longevity by asking pastors, churches and regional church leaders to commit themselves to encouraging longer early pastorates.

STRATEGY #7: Monitor Pastoral Transitions

Short-term pastorates are often inadvertently begun with an unsatisfactory transition from one church to another. Either the pastor chooses the wrong church, or the church chooses the wrong man. At least that is what they say when they part a couple of years later. However it happens, the entire process of moving pastors from one church to another can set the stage for shorter-than-desired pastorates. The strategy for dealing with this particular obstacle to longevity is to *monitor pastoral transitions.*

Just as it is expected that pastors will change churches and that churches will change pastors, it is also expected that the way those changes are made will continue as they have always been. And it is the way those transitions have always been made that needs monitoring. Who needs to monitor pastoral transitions? Everybody can help—pastors, churches and denominational leadership.

Monitoring begins by helping a pastor with his assessment of whether he should stay or leave. Some of the practical questions he can use include, "Have I been here long enough to reach my most effective years—in other words, have I been here more than six or seven years? Do I have a dream for this church? Do my spiritual gifts match the present needs of my position and church and will they fit for several years to come? Is my philosophy of ministry compatible with my church—do we work smoothly together? Does my social and cultural background fit this church or have we at least come to a good understanding on expectations, practices and traditions? Considering the opportunities facing the church, am I the right person to help it take advantage of these? Do I have a specialized ministry my church needs, or am I more of the generalist that my church needs? Is my credibility strong enough that people are willing to follow me in major decisions? Given my current situation, am I willing and able to work hard with my church? Is my leadership style generally what the church needs at this time?

To how many of these questions did you answer "yes"?

9 or 10: You need to stay.
7 or 8: Don't be looking for greener pastures just yet.
5 or 6: Stay around and work on the areas represented by your "no" answers.
3 or 4: Maybe you should start preparing your resume.
1 or 2: You should have already sent out your resume![12]

If you answered these questions about transition all by yourself, go back and ask them again, this time with some friends to help you monitor your answers.

Once the decision to leave has been made, then comes the easiest and at the same time the hardest part of the process—candidating. It is easy because whether your group uses an appointment or "call" system of placing pastors in churches, everyone likes to be courted. It is hard because there has never been and never will be a perfect pastor-parish fit. The task in this stage of monitoring pastoral transitions is to reduce the chances of a mismatch.

The pastor-parish fit instrument developed by Alban Institute is a good place to start. It is designed to help clergy measure the correct fit between themselves and their congregations. With some minor adjustments, it can also be used by the prospective pastor looking for a church. In addition, the American Baptist Personnel Services has developed an extensive questionnaire that can be used by churches to give a pastoral candidate as good an introduction to the church as possible (for these two resources, see bibliography entries 114, 118).

Because pastoral transitions based on the "weekend romance" model of candidating are always risky, I would encourage denominational leadership, pastoral search committees and candidating pastors to monitor the transition process with an eye to laying a better foundation for longer pastorates.

Part of that successful transition from one church to another is the first 12–18 months of ministry. Oswald calls these months a pastor's "point of entry" when he is entering new roles, new relationships and a new phase of one's ministry career. He suspects that "many ministries have been seriously hindered by the fact that the pastor and the parish did not get off to a good start." He assumes that the first 18 months of a new ministry will for the most part determine the entire ministry of a pastor in that particular local church.[13]

The bibliography contains several resources to help the pastor, church and regional leadership deal with such transition issues as seeing the importance of exiting a church properly as the foundation for one's next ministry and successfully entering a new work with longevity in mind (see entries 7, 26, 27, 38, 50, 51, 52, 80).

Churches and pastors have assumed for too long that the transition of clergy from one church to another is no big deal. It should be clear by now that this is wrong. If we want to see more pastors and churches staying together longer we need to start monitoring those transitions.

An Open Footnote toDenominational Leaders

Most of the pastors, laypeople and church leaders that I have talked to about pastoral longevity feel that regional leadership (in many denominations, the district superintendent) should do more to encourage longevity. Usually a regional leader serves mostly as a pastor to pastors, and does not get involved in local churches unless asked; but some leaders are seeing a need for intervention to break the short-term cycle in pastorates. This kind of involvement can be threatening to local pastors and churches and may not be recognized as a positive thing until after the fact, but it is one way to be more intentional about longevity.[14]

Churchman Norman Shawchuck agrees with this new role for denominational leadership. He has said that leaders need to talk about longevity, raise the expectations of pastors and laity and be more aggressive in dealing with the issues related to longevity.

Regional leaders are in the best position to influence pastors and churches toward the goal of longevity. Through in-service seminars for pastors and training for churches between pastors, regional leaders can increase the stability of many congregations for years to come.

Endnotes

1. Bruce Mawhinney, *Preaching with Freshness* (Eugene, OR: Harvest House, 1991), pp. 54–55.
2. Charles Spurgeon, *Lectures To My Students* (Grand Rapids, MI: Zondervan, 1954), p. 309.
3. H. Newton Maloney, "Ministerial Burnout," *Leadership*, Fall 1980, p. 72.
4. Stewart Pierson, "Keys To a Long Pastorate," *Leadership*, Spring 1984, p. 136.
5. Roy Oswald et al., *New Visions for the Long Pastorate* (Washington, DC: Alban Institute, 1983), p. 62.
6. Kevin Miller, *Secrets of Staying Power* (Waco, TX: Word, 1988), p. 157.
7. William Dyrness, *How Does America Hear the Gospel?* (Grand Rapids, MI: Eerdmans, 1989), p. 51.
8. Hobgood, William. "The Long-Tenured Pastorate: A Study of Ways to Build Trust," Unpublished Thesis, Lancaster (PA) Seminary, 1982, p. 91.

9. Lyle Schaller, *Survival Tactics in the Parish* (Nashville: Abingdon, 1977), pp. 185–190.

10. Lyle Schaller, *The Pastor and the People* (Nashville: Abingdon, 1973), pp. 10–11.

11. Lyle Schaller, *The Seven-Day-A-Week Church* (Nashville: Abingdon, 1992), p. 68.

12. Gary McIntosh, "Is It Time to Leave?" *Leadership*, Summer 1986, p. 70–75.

13. Roy Oswald, *New Beginnings: A Pastorate Start-up Workbook* (Washington, DC: Alban Institute, 1977), pp. 1– 2.

14. Hobgood, "The Long-Tenured Pastorate," pp. 93–94, 113.

· CHAPTER TEN ·

THE PLANNING

Dave (not his real name) had pastored three churches in 11 years. For those who may not be as quick as others, that averages out to about 3.7 years per church. His shortest pastorate was two years—one of those special, short-term assignments from the district superintendent when he was asked to bring a church into the denomination from another group.

Dave had never given much thought to longevity. So he accepted a call to his fourth church just as he had accepted the calls from two of the other pastorates. Just as he had done before, he came with no plans on leaving. And this time he stayed—for over 16 years. He stayed through the growth and the grumbling, through the building and the church fire, through the pressures and the pleasures.

If we were to ask Dave what he thinks about longevity now, he would say some of the very things you have already read. "You get to know people, they trust you, they see your consistency, it makes you dig to stay fresh, and it helps the church's identification with fringe families."

While Dave may not have planned for pastoral longevity, we can—and should. In the *Ministry Currents* issue dealing with "short-lived pastors," the authors from the Barna Research Group concluded,

> The plain truth is that the shorter the period of time a pastor has in which to operate, the less impact he or she is likely to have in that ministry. . . . When the pastor is constantly packing and unpacking the luggage, spending more time writing resumes than sermons, and more time meeting with search committees than ministering to hurting members of the body, ministry is compromised. You cannot maximize your potential if you are always looking over your shoulder. Plant your roots and engage in a long-term pastorate by leading the church to accomplish the special vision that God has ordained for that place, with you at the helm. Lead or get out of the way, indeed. But recognize that effective leadership is facilitated by a long-term commitment to a church.[1]

Pastors and churches need to be more intentional about staying together longer. While there may be some legitimate reasons for a pastor to leave (he is unwanted, untrusted or absolutely must have a fresh start) there are often reasons to consider staying longer (the people want him to stay, he wants to resolve some of the problems and leave on a high note or he feels he can have better results by staying).[2] Far too often, pastors and churches pay too little attention too late to what we have come to call the vow of stability.

SHORT-TERM SHOCK

Staying longer, longevity, the vow of stability—all these labels are the same as Alvin Toffler's "homing instinct," the in-bred desire of people to feel comfortable, safe and secure in familiar surroundings. In his classic best-seller *Future Shock*, he writes about the effect of mobility on people:

> For any relocation, of necessity, destroys a complex web-work of old relationships and establishes a set of new ones. It is this disruption that, especially if repeated more than once, breeds the 'loss of commitment' that many writers have noted among the high mobiles. The man on the move is ordinarily in too much of a hurry to put down roots in any one place. . . . Commitment, however, appears to correlate with duration of relationship. Armed with a culturally conditioned set of durational expectancies, we have all learned to invest with emotional content those relationships that appear to us to be "permanent" or relatively long-lasting, while withholding emotion, as much as possible, from short-term relationships. The declining commitment to place is thus related not to mobility per se, but to a concomitant of mobility—the shorter duration of relationships. . . . Across the board, the average interpersonal relationship in our life is shorter and shorter in duration.

And then he adds, "The knowledge that no move is final, that somewhere along the road the nomads will once more gather up their belongings and migrate, works against the development of relationships that are more than modular."[3] Toffler has pinpointed why we need to plan for pastoral longevity. In the midst of a society with a mobile mindset, ministry to people needs a context where there is commitment and relationships. And it won't happen by chance.

LONG-TERM MEGA-TREND?

We need to start thinking long-term instead of short-term. In fact, John Naisbitt, author of the best-selling book *Megatrends*, says we already have. Naisbitt sees a trend in the near future of moving away from short-term thinking to long-term thinking. He points to the world-wide criticism of American business and the short-term orientation of American business managers. The reward system in American business, he says, has recognized the short-term results. The average tenure of CEO's is about five years, with all of them wanting to make their mark in that short time frame.

"What gets lost is the strategy that will take the company over 25 to 30 years," Naisbitt adds. "Not one American corporation in ten has truly long-term (six to 10 years) compensation plans for its executives." Along with American business, the church has also failed to plan for the long-term.

"By contrast," Naisbitt continues, "Japanese managers pursue long-term strategies despite short-term costs . . . while we focus on numbers because we always focus on what we can measure. And numbers are short-term." Does this sound familiar? How many pastors pack up and move because the numbers aren't there? Isn't that the same kind of short-term thinking Naisbitt has seen in the corporate life of America?

Naisbitt's thoughts continue on a positive note: "Companies can change the signals that push their own people away from long-term vision into short-term myopia. . . . They can reaffirm the need for planning for the long haul."[4] That same admonishment can and should be made to pastors, churches and denominational leaders. We must reaffirm the need to "plan for the long haul."

Naisbitt goes on to say that companies wanting to reorient themselves to the long term rather than the short term must ask themselves, "What business are we really in?" He has seen too many companies that have developed a narrow definition of what they produce. For instance, railroad companies insist that they are in the "railroad" business instead of thinking long-term and saying they are in the transportation business. Such a change in philosophy could have enlarged their vision and produced longer-term thinking that would have saved them years of decline and financial crisis.

Pastors and churches need to ask themselves the same question. "What business are we in?" For too long the answers have been, the "preaching business" or the "church growth business" or the "career business" or the "education business." Instead, the answer should reflect longer-term thinking. We are in the *reconciliation* business, the *relationship* business, the *growing people* business. These kinds of answers can't help but stimulate creativity and energy for planning longevity.

We can and should start planning for longevity. We have already explored the obstacles to longevity and offered seven strategies to manage them. On the next several pages are charts showing the possibilities for planning for longevity. This is not the last word—these outlines and guidelines are presented to encourage you to add your own suggestions. Pastors and churches can plan to stay longer together.

If Toffler is right, short-term relationships produce "future shock"—not only in our society but in our pastors and churches. He advises us to "consciously assess our own life pace. Having done this, we can also begin consciously to influence it. . . . The rate of turnover in our lives, for example, can be influenced by conscious decisions." He says that we can "cut down on the change by maintaining longer-term relationships." He concludes by reminding us that "the problem is not, therefore, to suppress change, which cannot be done, but to manage it."[5]

So let's start managing the change of pastors and churches. When a former editor of *Leadership* resigned after 10 years, he offered the following advice to anyone wishing to manage their own moves. "Explore every possibility. Create a bias against leaving. Nothing on earth is forever, God is in control."[6]

What I have been trying to do in this book is "create a bias against leaving." I want us to think more about the vow of stability than ever before. We have greater control over longevity than we may realize. We are not victims of a system; we don't have to be stuck in a rut. While not every pastorate will be long-term, we must begin to make choices to manage our mobility and longevity—for the sake of our ministry and the church of Jesus Christ.

> I believe God wants us to be successful . . . and yet success is not always obvious. The Chinese bamboo tree does absolutely nothing—or so it seems—for the first four years. Then suddenly, sometime during the fifth year, it shoots up ninety feet in sixty days. Would you say that bamboo tree grew in six weeks, or five years? I think our lives are akin to that Chinese bamboo tree. Sometimes we put forth effort, put forth effort, and put forth effort . . . and nothing seems to happen. But if you do the right things long enough, you'll receive the rewards of your efforts.[7]

Endnotes

1. *Ministry Currents*, Barna Research Group, 1992, p. 6.
2. James Berkeley, *Making the Most of Mistakes* (Waco, TX: Word, 1987), pp. 98–107.
3. Alvin Toffler, *Future Shock* (Toronto/New York/London: Bantam, 1970), pp. 89, 93, 102, 105.
4. John Naisbitt, *Megatrends* (New York: Warner, 1982), pp. 81–101.
5. Toffler, *Future Shock,* pp. 375, 377.
6. Terry Muck, "The Back Page," *Leadership*, Spring 1990, p. 146.
7. S. Truett Cathy, *Leadership*, Summer 1986, p. 35.

OBSTACLES TO LONGEVITY	AGENCIES WHICH CAN TAKE STEPS OF ACTION			
	Educational Institutions	Pastors	Churches	District/Regional Leaders
Lack of Awareness	*Restoring the Vow of Stability*	*Restoring the Vow of Stability*	*Restoring the Vow of Stability*	*Restoring the Vow of Stability*
Lack of Continued Personal Growth	Unit on factors of continuing education	Develop personal program: reading 50 hours/year; sabbatical; "self-care"	Encourage pastoral continuing education	Provide continuing education experiences
Lack of Self-Awareness	Myers-Briggs; relate counseling/guidance to longevity	Myers-Briggs; *Church Leadership Kit*	Work with pastor on *Church Leadership Kit*	Seminars using *Church Leadership Kit*
Mismanagement of Conflict	Teach conflict management skills	Read suggested books *How to Manage Conflict Kit*	*Lay Persons' Guide to Conflict Management*; *How to Manage Conflict Kit*	Seminars using *How to Manage Conflict Kit*
Inadequate Pastor/Parish Relationship	Teach principles of *Pastor/Parish Committee*	Use of *Mutual Ministry Committee*	Use of *Mutual Ministry Committee*, use suggested books by Lavender and Bratcher	Assist churches and pastors in implementing pastor/parish committee
Faulty Early Patterns	Instruct for greater awareness of longevity	*Crossing the Boundaries* increase expectations	Increase awareness	Increase awareness; seminar for young men: "New Beginnings"
Faulty Pastoral Transitions		*Running through the Thistles*; Participate in "New Beginnings" group; *The Pastor as Newcomer*; Use "Pastor-Parish Fit"	*Developmental Tasks of a Church in Search of a Pastor,* Use "Pastor-Parish Fit" or forms from American Baptist	Initiate "New Beginnings" groups; work with church on their "developmental tasks"; teach church about pastor-parish relations committee; work with church using "Pastor-Parish Fit" or forms from the American Baptist

AGENCIES WHICH CAN CONTRIBUTE RESOURCES	STAGES IN A PASTOR'S LIFE TO APPLY RESOURCES			
	EDUCATION	FIRST CHURCH	CONFLICT	TRANSITION
Educational Institution	Study of Longevity Personal guidance counseling Myers-Briggs Conflict skills	*Crossing the Boundaries;* "New Beginnings" group; Develop self-awareness, conflict skills, awareness of longevity factors (especially "faulty early patterns")	Take course in conflict management; read suggested bibliography on conflict management	*The Pastor as Newcomer*
Pastor	Become aware of longevity; design self-study	Establish a "Pastor/Parish Relations Committee"; seek to overcome early faulty patterns; develop personal growth program	Initiate *How to Manage Conflict Kit* with church; read suggested bibliography on conflict management	Join a "New Beginnings" group; use "Pastor-Parish Fit" in candidating; encourage new church to establish a "Pastor/Parish Relations Committee"
Local Church	Provide models of pastoral longevity	Establish a "Pastor/Parish Relations Committee"; develop an awareness of longevity (use *Restoring the Vow of Stability*)	*How to Manage Conflict Kit; A Layperson's Guide to Conflict Management*	
District/Regional Leadership	Provide models of pastoral longevity for classroom use	Establish "New Beginnings" groups; help set up "Pastor/Parish Relations Committees"; use *Restoring the Vow of Stability* as a resource for awareness of longevity	Study the *How to Manage Conflict Kit* with pastors in a group setting	Establish a "New Beginnings" group; work with district or region on "Pastor-Parish Fit"

• APPENDIX A •

General Implications for Longevity from the New Testament Epistles

(Romans 1:12)

"That is, that you and I may be mutually encouraged by each other's faith." "Mutual ministry" can occur both in a short-term ministry as in Paul's relationship to the Romans, and in a long-term ministry. But it is deepened and enriched by longer association.

(Romans 12:10)

"Be devoted to one another in brotherly love. Honor one another above yourselves." While this can be true regardless of the time frame, it has more meaning in a longer-term ministry, in which the pastor is devoted to his people.

(1 Thessalonians 5:12–13)

"Now we ask you, brothers, to respect those who work hard among you, who are over you in the Lord and who admonish you. Hold them in the highest regard in love because of their work. Live in peace with each other." The tone of this passage suggests a relationship of some length between the leaders and the people. Those who "work hard" have been known to these people for some time.

(1 Timothy 3:7)

"He must also have a good reputation with outsiders, so that he will not fall into disgrace and into the devil's trap." An important qualification of an elder is his standing with those in the community. The implication is that he has been a part of that community for some time, long enough to have established a reputation.

(1 Timothy 5:22)

"Do not be hasty in the laying on of hands, and do not share in the sins of others. Keep yourself pure." By the end of the first century, it took three years for a person to become a member of the church. It took time for the people to get to know the person's life. The longer a person was around, the better they knew him.

(2 Timothy 1:18)

"May the Lord grant that he [Onesiphorus] will find mercy from the Lord on that day! You know very well in how many ways he helped me in Ephesus." A man needs to have his ministry known, that is, people need to see him in ministry long enough to have trust in him.

(Titus 1:5)

"The reason I left you in Crete was that you might straighten out what was left unfinished and appoint elders in every town, as I directed you." The implication here is that elders were to be appointed in the city of their residence. The men would be known to the people by their long-term relationship with them prior to their appointment.

(Hebrews 5:2)

The analogy of Christ's ministry as a priest reflects on the role of the pastor as priest: "He is able to deal gently with those who are ignorant and are going astray, since he himself is subject to weakness." Such knowledge comes with knowing people for a time. In the interviews referred to earlier, it was often mentioned that a pastor can get to know his people better, get into their heart and life, to let them know who he is and find out who they are. That depth of ministry can be meaningful.

(Hebrews 6:1)

"Therefore let us leave the elementary teachings about Christ and go on to maturity, not laying again the foundation of repentance from acts that lead to death, and of faith in God." With a longer-term ministry, a man doesn't have to lay the basic foundation of truth, but can move on to in-depth teaching. One of the complaints of having a series of short-term pastors is that the basics get repeated over and over again, rather than moving on into deeper truths.

(Hebrews 13:7)

"Remember your leaders, who spoke the word of God to you. Consider the outcome of their way of life and imitate their faith." Those who were to be imitated had lived long enough among the people so that their example was known.

(Hebrews 13:17)

"Obey your leaders and submit to their authority. They keep watch over you as men who must give an account. . . ." With a longer pastorate, the pastor can know his people better, and give a better "account."

(James 3:1)

"Not many of you should presume to be teachers, my brothers, because you know that we who teach will be judged more strictly." The unspoken implication is that the teachers came from within the assembly of believers. They were approved and appointed by the Christian community. Even into the early centuries of the church, the laity were active in calling out from among them leaders already known to them, though this declined over the years.[1] This dynamic would be best repeated today in longer-term pastorates.

(1 Peter 5:2–3)

"Be shepherds of God's flock that is under your care, serving as overseers—not because you must, but because you are willing, as God wants you to be; not greedy for money, but eager to serve; not lording it over those entrusted to you, but being examples to the flock." We have already referred to the image of the shepherd used by Peter in talking about the ministry of the pastor-elder.

(2 Peter 2:1)

"But there were also false prophets among the people, just as there will be false teachers among you. . . ." The opposite would also be true: true prophets would arise from among the people, a point mentioned above.

(1 John 1:3)

"We proclaim to you what we have seen and heard, so that you also may have fellowship with us. . . ." The goal of proclamation was not additional knowledge, but "koinonia" with those who did the teaching. "Koinonia" can occur better as people get to know each other over longer periods of time.

(1 John 2:19)

"They went out from us, but they did not really belong to us. For if they had belonged to us, they would have remained with us; but their going showed that none of them belonged to us."Again, the implication is that teachers arose from among the people, a dynamic only duplicable in a longer-term ministry.

(2 John 1:5)

"And now, dear lady, I am not writing you a new command but one we have had from the beginning. I ask that we love one another." John was able to write his instruction based upon a previous relationship with his reader. The better and longer the relationship, the more effective the words of instruction.

(2 John 1:10)

"If anyone comes to you and does not bring this teaching, do not take him into your house or welcome him." Even though John is talking about itinerant preachers, the problem of short-term knowledge of a person affects the "ethos" of the preacher.

(2 John 1:12)

"I have much to write to you, but I do not want to use paper and ink. Instead, I hope to visit you and talk with you face to face, so that our joy may be complete." Here and in Third John 1:13, John prefers a face-to-face encounter. The emphasis on personal relationship in ministry favors the longer-term ministry.

(3 John 1:8)

"We ought therefore to show hospitality to such men [traveling preachers of truth]. . . ." John recognizes there is a place for this type of ministry. Demetrius was a good example of this (1:12).

Endnotes

1. Cheslyn Jones, Geoffrey Wainwright and Edward Yarnold, S.J., *Study of Liturgy* (New York: Oxford University Press, 1978), pp. 295, 303, 311, 316, 321.

· APPENDIX B ·

Observations from Interviews

During my research for this book, I spent several months meeting with and interviewing dozens of lay people, pastors and church leaders. Each interview was taped for further analysis. Each observation was recorded for later study.

I have reported my conclusions from the study below. These summations are made in no specific order of importance. Several of these observations have already been included in the body of this book. These conclusions are presented to be a helpful starting point for further contributions to the challenge of pastoral longevity.

1. Short-term churches are hurting churches, suffering from self-image problems. They often have doubts about themselves, their performance and their suitability for a pastor. A defensive attitude was detected in several lay people representing short-term churches, even to the point of denying that long-term was preferable over short-term pastorates. Short-term churches tended to ask questions like, "What is wrong with us?" and to experience some of the grief reaction common to other types of human loss. Some had the self-image of unworthiness or saw their role in the district as just helping young pastors get started, thus unable to expect a man to stay very long in their church.

Short-term churches also appeared to be confused, guilt-ridden, damaged and pained. Though the leaving of a man is considered a traumatic event, they often feel that their pastors leave the church too soon.

2. The general impression among churches, pastors and laypeople in my own denomination—The Christian and Missionary Alliance—is that the Alliance has a reputation for short-term pastorates. It appeared that many people did not know that men stayed longer than four to five years. The general consensus was, however, that there was a need and a desire to increase longevity among Alliance pastors and churches. In some cases, that feeling has intensified over the years, even to the point of some being opposed to short-term rather strongly.

3. When it came to defining what "long-term" was and what people expected, there was some confusion. Some people needed "long-term" defined while others were unsure as to whether it meant five years or more. Most Christian and Missionary Alliance laypeople do not expect a pastor to stay longer than five years. Their previous experience has formed this expectation for the most part. Though a church may want long-term pastorates, they have come not to expect them.

4. Emphasis on the matching of pastor to people received some attention. Most of the comments centered around the desirability of a fit (educationally, background, etc.) and the fact that it usually takes both the church and the man a couple of tries to find that match. This is evidently supposed to explain the frequent changing of pastors from church to church. One respondent discounted the idea of "the perfect pastor for the perfect church," feeling that this was the cause of a lot of

unnecessary moving around.

5. Opinions about what makes longevity happen were varied. There appeared to be a general feeling that "it just happens" without being able to tell how to make it happen until it has happened. When the question about the advantages of a longer pastorate was asked, short-term pastors made 10 responses, and short-term churches made 13 responses, while long-term pastors made 30 responses and long-term churches made 18 responses. When the question was asked, "What contributes to longer pastorates?" short-term pastors and churches made 11 and 14 responses respectively, while long-term pastors and churches made 42 and 32 responses respectively. Some felt that it was as much the pastor's responsibility as it was the church's responsibility.

6. There was little doubt as to what led to short-term pastorates. Among the items listed were conflicts, stress, family needs, a need for a new challenge, new goals and various practical issues. There was a minimal number of advantages listed for short-term ministries, as compared to the advantages of a long-term ministry. The comparison of responses is as follows:

- Number of responses to advantages of long-term, 74;
- Number of responses to advantages of short-term, 23;
- Number of responses to disadvantages of long-term, 28;
- Number of responses to disadvantages of short-term, 39.

7. Lack of assistance from educational institutions was evident. Those who commented gave evidence of a negative modeling and instruction in this area of ministry preparation. One person received all of his ideas about longevity totally outside of the

classroom. The major concepts that schools gave to pastoring and moving were that a man should expect to move often (thus, time spent on the candidating procedure) and the "stepping-stone" approach to pastoral placement and relocation.

8. The importance of early patterns became evident. It seems that the pastor's early experience will often set the stage for duplication later on, whether for longer-term or shorter-term. Churches exhibit the same tendency to repeat previous patterns in length of pastors' stays. It was mentioned that when a church deliberately looks for a man who will stay longer, they look for a man who has a record of staying longer.

9. Of interest to note are the two images used to describe the pastor leaving/staying. The two images most often used were that of the marriage model and the father-child model.

10. There was a realistic look taken at longevity as well. It was recognized that longevity is not for everyone, nor is it the most important thing. Long-term churches can plateau, and short-term churches can grow. Long-term churches can become comfortable and in a rut, while short-term churches can be infused from time to time with new life. Some concern was expressed regarding the issue of replacing a long-term pastor when he leaves.

11. Opinions varied as to how long a man should stay. Some preferred nebulous terms like "as long as he is effective" or other non-committal answers. Most people felt that a four-to-seven-year ministry was acceptable, while some held the opinion that a man ought to stay 12–15 years on average. Only a few felt that a man should stay as few as three years.

12. The transition period for pastors and churches to get to know each other was generally agreed to be a minimum of three years. It takes longer for a man to get to know the community beyond the church.

13. The self-image of the pastor entered the discussion at several stages. "Advancement" was an admitted pressure that most of the men felt in one form or another. One man said that he didn't play "the denominational game" of ladder-climbing. Others looked to personal growth to satisfy this need for advancement. The comment was made that the district ought to find some way to give men a feeling of worth without the man having to candidate somewhere else to feel wanted.

14. Among the important contributors to longevity are:

- long-range goals set by both church and pastor;
- a shared ministry, in which the pastor is not at the center;
- openness and flexibility by the pastor and people;
- a "fit"—a common philosophy of ministry;
- willingness to work through problems and mistakes;
- mutual ministry of encouragement and appreciation between pastor and people;
- providing for the pastor financially;
- perception by pastor and people of the value of long-term;
- an open and working relationship between the pastor and board;
- a ministry into the community.

15. Among the advantages of a long-term pastorate are:

- "depth" ministry of pastor to people;
- getting to know people and community;
- ability to set and reach long-range goals;
- experiencing the cycles of life together, and learning to work through them together;
- its positive effect on the personal growth of the pastor as well as the church.

16. Among the primary reasons for pastors leaving, conflicts was listed. This same theme will be found in the suggestions made on how to increase longevity. But it is interesting to note that not only did pastors and churches have an inability to work through conflict, but in several places, it became apparent that district superintendents and other denominational leaders would also benefit by training in conflict management.

17. The church's reputation in the community is affected by a series of short-term pastors. It can become an embarrassment to local church members when they are asked by friends in the community "Well, who is your pastor now?" Longer-term pastors bring stability to the church. One misconception about short-term pastors was corrected: instead of providing the church with a well-rounded program through several pastors, what can result is a hodgepodge of disconnected programs.

18. It was the opinion of some that the larger churches could expect a man to stay longer, as could rural churches (the pressures in the city causing men to move more frequently). In addition, a man with a growing family eventually will want to look for a place to settle down with that family and is more likely to be longer-term. In one case, the comment was made that a congregation with an older median age prefers a more stable

man who will stay longer.

19. There was some question as to whether "longevity" was a biblical concept or not. One person said he doubted that it was, while several others said they could find no precedent in Scripture for pastors moving. It will be important to develop a biblical understanding of this issue. One concept of ministry directly related to longevity is the nature of ministry and relationships. It becomes clear that longer-term ministries enhance deeper relationships, which provide a good foundation for ministry in relationships (a biblical theme).

20. While "newness" and "ability to perform one task well" were given as advantages to short-term, the disadvantages outweighed the advantages (39–23 in responses). Among the disadvantages were:

- people become resistant to new ideas (which is the very advantage often listed);
- church loses people with each pastor leaving;
- adjusting to a new man all the time, the church loses time in developing a community ministry;
- same basic themes covered by each man.

21. Some of the items that were considered to contribute to shorter pastorates were:

- people didn't expect the man to stay long;
- pastor in need of more financial support;
- inability to handle conflict/mistakes/pressure;
- lack of long-term goals;
- lack of ordination (if a man was ordained, the people and

the man would be less likely to treat the pastorate as a "training" pastorate);
• man looking for another place that offered what the present church did not.

22. A profile of a man who tends to be short-term emerges as being:

• impatient for change in the church;
• lazy (not willing to work at in-depth ministry);
• limited in gifts (able to do one thing well and then move on to do it again in another church);
• unable to change leadership style—tends to be task-oriented;
• has no plans of staying longer than previous pastorates.

23. In general, neither the long-term pastors nor the sort-term pastors initially planned on how long they were going to stay in a particular church, although more of the long-term men grew to that conviction in their long-term ministry. It seems that, in general, most pastors and churches have given little thought to the issue of pastoral longevity (some admitted that they hadn't thought about it until asked to do so by my project).

24. Widespread was the desire to redesign the candidating process. At times, churches need greater assistance from district or regional leadership, as does the individual pastor. A church and a pastor can overreact to a previous situation in making a new selection. Too often pastors move in the midst of conflict, which doesn't surface again until the new man has been installed for a while in the church. In addition to the general lack of expectations regarding longevity, often district or regional

leadership encourages men to move too soon.

25. While longer-term ministries have their admitted disadvantages (ruts, too comfortable, flat spots in the church's ministry, difficulty of leaving after being there for so many years and church recovery after a long-term man), the general consensus is that long-term is preferable to short-term. Most short-term pastors did not like the short-term ministry, and neither did the churches. Short-term ministries were hard on the pastor and the church. The pressure to take the path of least resistance comes from society around us. Yet all expressed the need to increase the potential of pastoral longevity.

APPENDIX C

The Use of the Myers-Briggs Type Indicator

The Myers-Briggs Type Indicator is a temperament styles inventory that has its roots in Carl Jung's theory of types. Jung's original theory said that there are four basic behavioral traits to be found, in particular kinds of combinations, in all human beings. "Sensation establishes what is actually given, thinking enables us to recognize its meaning, feelings tell us its value, and finally, intuition points to the whence and whither that lie within the immediate facts."[1]

Jung meant that one's primary temperament cannot be both thinking and feeling, nor could one be both sensing and intuitive, while one can be thinking and sensing or thinking and intuitive, or feeling with either sensing or intuitive. Others (notably Jung's granddaughter, Isabel Myers) have expanded on the jungian theory and, in the Myers-Briggs Type Indicator, have made it a viable way of seeing oneself in relation to others.

The Indicator adds, in addition to the two pairs identified above, two others: extraversion/introversion and judging/perceiving. The definitions of the polarities that this Indicator offers are:

> Extroversion: you relate more easily to the other world of people and things than to the inner world of ideas.

Sensing: you would rather work with known facts than look for possibilities and relationships.

Thinking: you base your judgment more on impersonal analysis and logic than on personal values.

Judging: you like a planned, decided, orderly way of life better than a flexible, spontaneous way.

Introversion: you relate more easily to the inner world of ideas than to the outer world of people and things.

Intuition: you would rather work for possibilities and relationships than work with known facts.

Feelings: you base your judgments on personal values rather than on impressional analysis and logic.

Perceiving: you like a flexible, spontaneous way of life better than a planned, decided and orderly way.

One can, in taking the Myers-Briggs Type Indicator, emerge with any combination of the items in the left column with those in the right. On any one of the four polarities, one will be either to the left or the right of center. Two other people have done extensive work with the Indicator and have developed its usefulness further. After testing a wide enough field to be statistically predictable, David Kiersey and Marilyn Bates have identified four basic temperament styles as the fundamental possibilities for all human beings. Each of these is a pair of polarities (excluding extroversion-introversion). Put another way, every person is either sensing-judging, sensing-perceiving, intuitive-thinking or intuitive-feeling.

In the general population, 12 percent are of the intuitive-feeling type (NF). "NF" people tend to make decisions with personal warmth. But since they prefer intuition, their interest is not in facts, but in possibilities, things which have not happened, new possibilities for people. They tend to be very aware of other people and their feelings, enjoy pleasing people, like harmony, often let decisions be influenced by their own or other people's likes and wishes, need occasional praise, dislike telling people unpleasant things, are more people-oriented, tend to be sympathetic, work in bursts of enthusiasm with slack periods in between, like solving new problems, reach a conclusion quickly, are impatient with routine and details, follow their inspirations (good or bad) and frequently make errors of fact.

In the general population, 38 percent are of the sensing-perceiving type (SP). "SP" people dislike new problems unless there are standard ways to solve them, like an established way of doing things, work more steadily with a realistic idea of how long it will take, are patient with routine details, are not often inspired and rarely trust the inspiration when they are, tend to be good at precise work, adapt well to changing situations, do not mind leaving things open for alterations, may have trouble making decisions, may start too many projects and have difficulty finishing them and may postpone unpleasant jobs.

In the general population, 38 percent are of the sensing-judging type (SJ). "SJ" people work best when they can plan their work and follow the plan, like to get things settled first, may decide things too quickly, may dislike to interrupt the project they are on for a more urgent one, may not notice new things that need to be done, want only the essentials needed to begin their work, tend to be satisfied once they reach a judgment on a thing, a situation or person, seldom make errors of fact, enjoy using skills already learned more than learning new ones, usually reach a conclusion step by step, are impatient when the details get too complicated and tend to be good at precise work.

In the general population, 12 percent are of the intuitive-thinking type (NT). "NT" people do not show emotion readily and are often uncomfortable dealing with people's feelings, may hurt people's feelings without knowing it, like analysis and putting things into logical order, can get along without harmony, tend to decide impersonally (sometimes paying insufficient attention to people's wishes), need to be treated fairly, are able to reprimand people or fire them when necessary, are more analytically oriented, respond more easily to people's thoughts, tend to be firm-minded, dislike doing the same thing repeatedly, reach a conclusion quickly and are patient with complicated situations.[2]

In a research and training workshop for long-tenured pastors and their spouses it was discovered that, although only 12 percent of the general population are "NF" people, 48 percent of the pastors in the workshop were of this temperament. Furthermore, *every* pastor in the group was "feeling" in temperament which means either "NF" or "SFJ" (sensing-feeling-judging) or "SFP" (sensing-feeling-perceiving).[3]

It begins to become clear that those who last long in pastorates are persons whose primary orientation is toward feeling-level interactions, who focus much of their energy and life on persons, and who thus become quite near to, and even intimate with their parishioners.

This is in sharp contrast to the findings of Speed Leas in a study of involuntary terminations of pastorates, in which one major conclusion is that clergy are fired because some of the laity experience the pastor as not liking them as persons.[4] It appears that pastors with long tenure derive "staying power" from deep involvement with persons, but it must be asked if at least some capacity to lead "the people" has been sacrificed in order to relate effectively to individual persons. There can be a high cost in a person-centered pastorate, for the very quality that most often enables a pastor to remain in one pastorate may also render the corporate and institutional part of that pastorate's life less and less creative and effective (see the discussion of the "Gap Theory" in chapter two).[5]

In their study of long-tenured pastorates, the Alban Institute concluded that:

> By far the majority of clergy attracted to a long pastorate are feeling oriented people. It is our experience that feeling oriented people are more vulnerable to the development of a "gap" in a long pastorate than thinking oriented people.
>
> Out of a total of seventy-two clergy in a pastorate of ten years or more, 90.5% emerged on the feeling side of the Myers-Briggs Type Indicator. The Center for Application of Psychological Type possesses research data that indicates that in the profession of clergy "F's" (feeling oriented persons) outnumber "T's" (thinking oriented persons) by as many as three to one.
>
> This high proportion . . . makes sense when one gives it some thought:
>
> - feeling types tend to become very attached to people and communities.
> - feeling types have a more difficult time saying "goodbye." At times the skill of a feeling oriented person serves a parish well over the long haul.
> - feeling types are much more in touch with people when

they are hurt and upset, are motivated to try to do something about the hurt or upset and usually have the skills to heal these pains.

On the liability side, feeling type clergy tend to enjoy working with people rather than with administrative detail. They have a greater tendency to slide into effective pastoral ministries, allowing organizational issues related to health and growth to go by the board. Feeling oriented clergy, following their natural inclinations, spend more time and energy on interpersonal relations than they do on corporate issues or on cold and impersonal organizational concerns. When a parish focuses on strong directional goals, some people will naturally be disturbed. The feeling oriented pastor will feel their pain much more acutely than a thinking oriented pastor.

Thinking type clergy tend to be more goal and competence oriented and to press organizational concerns, yet to be less aware of the feelings of people in the change effort. Being more competence oriented, and having less difficulty with farewells, once certain objectives have been fulfilled, they tend to move on to new challenges in other parishes. We surmise that they would be less capable of surviving a long pastorate because they have fewer skills and capabilities in identifying and dealing with discontent or hurt feelings in the parish. Should they have skills to compensate for this deficiency, they would be well suited for an effective long pastorate with their ability to keep growth and organizational issues moving.

In addition to the "F" function in these clergy, we also noted a higher than normal proportion of judging types than perceiving types. Of clergy tested, 71.9% favored judging over perceiving, an indication that these clergy value structure and order more than they do spontaneity and openness. Once again this strength they bring to their ministries in terms of stability and continuity can become their liability in their undervaluing change and renewal.

In the Alban Institute Interim Pastorate Project, we also built a profile of clergy best suited for Interim ministries (six to eighteen months preparation of congregations for more permanent ministers). These clergy were desirous of adventure, very goal oriented, comfortable with conflict, bored with long-term ministries and living in a style congruent with such short-term ministry.

If interim clergy are "hillside people," then clergy in long pastorates might be termed "pondside people" who build their homes over a pond where hills slope gently down to focus attention on a small, specific piece of real estate. These folks are continually fascinated by life right under their noses, intrigued with new forms of life revealed in day to day living, caught up in the dramas of the life of the pond, constantly plumbing the depth in the meaning of the life around them.

In the future we hope to develop a survey instrument to measure clergy's propensity to be either "hillside" or "pondside" pastors. This might help clergy plan their careers in a more informed way and assist them to come to terms with phenomena which occur in frequent moves or in long pastorates.[6]

John Davis, Executive Director of the North Central Career Development Center, New Brighton, Minnesota, uses the Myers-Briggs Type Indicator in describing the type of men who choose various styles of ministries. Most "evangelist-types" are "SF's"—their role centers around being an evangelist, and usually there are only so many people they can relate to. The "ST" and "NT" types are the "prophetic pastors," who tend to be harsh and don't wear well. The "NF" types are the "pastoral" pastors. They emphasize nurturing, discipling, and they tend to last longer. Davis estimated that from his experience, 60 percent of the clergy are "NF," 30 percent are "SF" and 10 percent are "ST" or "NT."

In summary, with the use of the Myers-Briggs Type Indicator, the man who is more likely to be a longer-term pastor is the "feeling" type, who gets more attached to people, finds it unthinkable to move, is more likely to settle into a particular pastoral ministry even after the goals are met, yet whose very sensitivity to people may get in the way of his ability to deal with the harder issues of parish life that must be dealt with if he is to last longer. The "thinking" type of pastor is more objective and goal-oriented and often gets restless after his goals are achieved. The "thinker" often satisfies the need to find new goals to sustain the challenge by moving to another church, rather than staying and developing new challenges where he is.

Endnotes

1. Carl Jung, *Modern Man in Search of a Soul* (NY: Harcourt, Brace & World, 1933), p. 93.
2. Isabel Myers-Briggs, *Introduction to Type* (Gainesville, FL: Center for Application of Psychological Type, 1962).
3. William Hobgood, "The Long-Tenured Pastorate: A Study of Ways to Build Trust," Unpublished Thesis, Lancaster (PA) Seminary, 1982, p. 9.
4. Speed Leas, *Should the Pastor Be Fired* (Washington, DC: Alban Institute, 1980), p. 5.
5. Hobgood, "The Long-Tenured Pastorate," pp. V–IX.
6. Roy Oswald et al., *New Visions for the Long Pastorate* (Washington, DC: Alban Institute, 1983), pp. 50–56.

BIBLIOGRAPHY

*(The bibliography is numbered to coincide
wth the suggested resources in chapter nine.)*

Books

1. Anderson, Leith. *A Church for the 21st Century.* Minneapolis, MN: Bethany, 1992.

2. Beker, J. Christian. *Paul the Apostle.* Philadelphia: Fortress Press, 1980.

3. Benjamin, Paul. *The Equipping Ministry.* Cincinnati: Standard Publishing, 1978.

4. Berkeley, James D. *Making the Most of Mistakes.* Waco, TX: Word, 1987.

5. Branson, Roy. *Church Split.* Bristol, TN: Landmark Publications, 1990.

6. Bratcher, Edward. *The Walk on the Water Syndrome.* Waco, TX: Word, 1984.

7. Bratcher, Edward, Robert Kemper, and Douglas Scott. *Mastering Transitions.* Portland, OR: Multnomah, 1991.

8. Carlson, Dwight. *Run and Not Be Weary.* Old Tappan, NJ: Revell, 1974.

9. Cousins, Don, Leith Anderson, and Arthur DeKruyter.

Mastering Church Management. Portland, OR: Multnomah, 1990.

10. DeVaux, Roland. *Ancient Israel—Religious Institutions.* 2 vols. New York/Toronto: McGraw-Hill, 1965.

11. Dunham, Marie, Gordon MacDonald and Donald Mc-Cullough. *Mastering Personal Growth.* Sisters, OR: Multnomah, 1992.

12. Dobson, Edward et al. *Mastering Conflict and Controversy.* Waco, TX: Word, 1992.

13. Dyrness, William. *How Does America Hear the Gospel?* Grand Rapids, MI: Erdmans, 1989.

14. Fletcher, John C. *Religious Authenticity in Clergy.* Washington, DC: Alban Institute, 1975.

15. Friesen, Gary. *Decision-Making and the Will of God.* Portland, OR: Multnomah, 1980.

16. George, Carl and Robert Logan. *Leading and Managing Your Church.* Old Tappan, NJ: Revell, 1987.

17. Gillaspie, Gerald. *The Restless Pastor.* Chicago: Moody, 1974.

18. Glasse, James. *Putting It Together in the Parish.* Nashville: Abingdon, 1972.

19. Grider, Edgar. *Can I Make It One More Year?* Atlanta: Knox, 1980.

20. Harrison, Everett F. *The Apostolic Church.* Grand Rapids, MI: Eerdmans, 1985.

21. Harrison, Roland K. *Introduction to the Old Testament.* Grand Rapids, MI: Eerdmans, 1969.

22. Hull, Bill. *The Disciple-Making Pastor.* Old Tappan, NJ: Revell, 1988.

23. Hulme, William et al. *Pastors in Ministry.* Minneapolis: Augsburg, 1985.

24. Jones, Cheslyn et al. *Study of Liturgy.* NY: Oxford University Press, 1978.

25. Jung, Carl. *Modern Man in Search of a Soul.* New York: Harcort, Brace, & World, Inc., 1933.

26. Ketcham, Bunty. *So You're on the Search Committee.* Washington, DC: Alban Institute, 1985.

27. Kirk, Richard J. *On the Calling and Care of Pastors.* Washington, DC: Alban Institute, 1973.

28. Kraft, Charles. *Christianity in Culture.* Maryknoll, NY: Orbis Books, 1980.

29. Lavender, Lucille. *They Cry, Too.* New York: Hawthorn Books, 1976.

30. Leas, Speed. *Discover Your Conflict Management Style.* Washington, DC: Alban Institute, 1979.

31. _____. *A Lay Person's Guide To Conflict Management.* Washington, DC: Alban Institute, 1979.

32. _____. *Moving Your Church Through Conflict.* Washington, DC: Alban Institute, 1985.

33. _____. *Should the Pastor Be Fired.* Washington, DC: Alban Institute, 1980.

34. _____. and Paul Kittlau. *Church Fights.* Philadelphia: Westminister Press, 1973.

35. Lightfoot, J.B., *The Apostolic Fathers.* Grand Rapids, MI: Baker Book House, 1956.

36. Ligon, Bill. *Discipleship: The Jesus View.* Plainfield, NJ: Logos International, 1979.

37. Mawhinney, Bruce. *Preaching with Freshness.* Eugene, OR:

Harvest House, 1991.

38. Mead, Loren. *The Developmental Tasks of the Congregation in Search of a Pastor.* Washington, DC: Alban Institute, 1977.

39. McKenna, David. *Renewing Our Ministry.* Waco, TX: Word, 1986.

40. Mickey, Paul and James Wilson. *Conflict and Resolution.* Nashville: Abingdon, 1973.

41. Miller, Calvin. *The Philippian Fragment.* Downers Grove, IL: InterVarsity Press, 1982.

42. Miller, Kevin. *Secrets of Staying Power.* Waco, TX: Word, 1988.

43. *Mutual Ministry Workbook.* Philadelphia, PA: Division of Professional Leadership, n.d.

44. Myers-Briggs, Isabel. *Introduction to Type.* Gainesville, FL: Center for Applications of Psychological Type, Inc., 1962.

45. Naisbitt, John. *Megatrends.* NY: Warner Books, 1982.

46. Ortiz, Juan. *Disciple.* Carol Stream, IL: Creation House, 1975.

47. Ortlund, Anne and Ray. *You Don't Have to Quit.* Nashville: Thomas Nelson, 1986.

48. Osborne, Larry. *The Unity Factor.* Waco, TX: Word, 1989.

49. Oswald, Roy. *Crossing the Boundaries: Meeting the Challenge of the First Years of Ministry.* Washington, DC: Alban Institute, 1986.

50. _____. *New Beginnings: A Pastorate Start Up Workbook.* Washington, DC: The Alban Institute, 1977.

51. _____. *The Pastor as Newcomer.* Washington, DC: Alban Institute, 1977.

52. _____. *Running Through the Thistles.* Washington, DC: Alban Institute, 1978.

53. _____ et al. *New Visions for the Long Pastorate.* Washington, DC: Alban Institute, 1983.

54. Perry, Lloyd. *Getting the Church on Target.* Chicago: Moody Press, 1977.

55. Peterson, Eugene. *The Contemplative Pastor.* Waco, TX: Word, 1989.

56. Ragsdale, Ray. *The Mid-Life Crises of a Minister.* Waco, TX: Word, 1978.

57. Rediger, G. Lloyd. *Coping With Clergy Burnout.* Valley Forge, PA: Judson Press, 1982.

58. Robbins, Paul. *When It's Time to Move.* Waco, TX: Word, 1985.

59. Rouch, Mark. *Competent Ministry.* Nashville: Abingdon, 1974.

60. Salter, Darius. *What Really Matters in Ministry.* Grand Rapids, MI: Baker, 1990.

61. Schaller, Lyle. *Activating the Passive Church.* Nashville: Parthenon Press, 1981.

62. _____. *The Change Agent.* Nashville: Abingdon, 1972.

63. _____. *Hey, That's Our Church.* Nashville: Abingdon, 1975.

64. _____. *It's a Different World.* Nashville: Abingdon, 1988.

65. _____. *The Middle-Sized Church.* Nashville: Abingdon, 1985.

66. _____. *The Multiple Staff and the Larger Church.* Nashville: Abingdon, 1980.

67. _____. *The Pastor and the People*. Nashville: Abingdon, 1973.

68. _____. *Reflections of a Contrarian*. Nashville: Abingdon, 1989.

69. _____. *The Seven-Day-A-Week Church*. Nashville: Abingdon, 1992.

70. _____. *Survival Tactics in the Parish*. Nashville: Abingdon, 1977.

71. Schuller, Robert. *Your Church Has Real Possibilities*. Glendale, CA: Gospel Light, 1974.

72. Shelley, Marshall. *Well-intentioned Dragons: Ministering to Problem People in the Church*. Waco, TX: Word, 1984.

73. Sine, Tom. *The Mustard Seed Conspiracy*. Waco, TX: Word, 1981.

74. Sparks, James Allen. *Potshots at the Preacher*. Nashville: Abingdon, 1977.

75. Spurgeon, Charles. *Lectures to My Students*. Grand Rapids, MI: Zondervan, 1954.

76. Stewart, Charles William. *Person and Profession*. Nashville: Abingdon, 1974.

77. Tillapaugh, Frank. *Unleashing the Church*. Ventura, CA: Regal, 1982.

78. Toffler, Alvin. *Future Shock*. Toronto/New York/London: Bantam Books, 1970.

79. Tucker, Michael. *The Church That Dared to Change*. Wheaton, IL: Tyndale, 1975.

80. Virkler, Henry. *Choosing a New Pastor: The Complete Handbook*. Nashville: Oliver-Nelson, 1992.

81. Wagner, C. Peter. *Your Church Can Grow.* Glendale, CA: Gospel Light, 1976.

82. _____. *Your Spiritual Gifts Can Help Your Church Grow.* Ventura, CA: Regal, 1979.

83. Watson, David. *I Believe in Evangelism.* Grand Rapid, MI: Eerdmans Publishing, 1976.

Articles

84. Anderson, Lynn. "Why I Have Stayed." *Leadership.* Summer 1986, pp. 79–80.

85. Bubna, Don. "Ten Reasons Not to Resign." *Leadership.* Fall 1983, p. 74.

86. Cardwell, Sue, and Richard Hunt. "Persistence in Seminary and Ministry." *Journal of Pastoral Psychology.* Winter 1979, pp. 119–131.

87. Cathy, S. Truett. *Leadership.* Summer 1986, p. 35.

88. Chromey, Rick. "Everything I Learned About Ministry, I Learned Dating My Wife." *Leadership.* Spring 1992, p. 21.

89. Ellison, Craig. "Where Does It Hurt?" *Leadership.* Spring 1982, p. 107.

90. Maloney, H. Newton. "Ministerial Burnout." *Leadership.* Spring 1984, p. 72.

91. McIntosh, Gary. "Is It Time to Leave?" *Leadership.* Summer 1986, p. 70–75.

92. McMullin, Stephen. "In the Pastoral Pastorate." *Leadership.* Summer 1987, p. 73.

93. Miller Cavin. "Fiddlin' with the Staff." *Leadership.* Winter 1986, p. 104.

94. Muck, Terry. "The Back Page." *Leadership.* Spring 1990, p. 146.

95. Nauss, Allen. "The Relation of Pastoral Mobility to Effectiveness." *Review of Religious Research.* Winter 1974, pp. 80–86.

96. _____ and Coiner, Harry. "The First Parish: Stayers and Movers." *Review of Religious Research.* Winter 1971, pp. 95–101.

97. Oswald, Roy. "The Pastor's Passages." *Leadership.* Fall 1983, pp. 12–17.

98. Palmberg, Burdette. "The Breaking of a Minister." *Leadership.* Summer 1986, p. 60.

99. Peterson, Eugene. "The Jonah Syndrome." *Leadership.* Summer 1990, p. 41–43.

100. _____. "Haphazardly Intent: An Approach to Pastoring." *Leadership.* Winter 1981, p. 12.

101. Pierson, Stewart. "Keys to a Long Pastorate." *Leadership.* Spring 1984, p. 136.

102. Price, Roy. "When the Pastor Gets Fired." *Leadership.* Fall 1983, p. 50.

103. Ramsey, Bonnie. "Christian Workers Are Programmed for Poverty." *Moody Monthly.* June 1976, pp. 80–81.

104. Reader, Harvey. "Why Most Pastors Are Rehabbers." *Leadership.* Fall 1987, p. 27.

105. Robinson, Haddon. "What Authority Do We Have Now?" *Leadership.* Spring 1992, p. 29.

106. Schaller, Lyle. "Whatever Happened to the Baby Boomers?" *The Journal of the Minister's Personal Library.* Volume VI, Number 1.

107. Shelley, Marshall and Kevin Miller, eds. "Secrets of Staying Power." *Leadership.* Summer 1986, p. 18.

108. "Shepherds Who Have Stayed." *Leadership*. Fall 1983, pp. 131–142.

109. Sorenson, Stephen. "Moving Targets: Ministry in a Transient Society." *Leadership*. Fall 1991, p. 123.

110. Stevens, R. Paul. "People in Print." *Leadership*. Fall 1985, p. 98.

111. Trollinger, William. "Riley's Empire." *Best in Theology III*. 1989, p. 118.

112. Wimberly, Ronald. "Mobility in Ministerial Career Patterns: Exploration." *Journal for the Scientific Study of Religion*. Vol. 10, 1971, pp. 249–253.

Other

113. *Church Leadership Kit*. Available from Spiritual Growth Resources, P.O. Box 971, Indianapolis, Indiana 46206.

114. *Church Questionnaire*. Valley Forge, PA: American Baptist Personnel Services.

115. Hobgood, William. "The Long-Tenured Pastorate: A Study of Ways to Build Trust." Unpublished Thesis for Lancaster Seminary (1982) Lancaster, PA.

116. Kack, George. "Staff Support Committee." Chicago: Evangelical Lutheran Church in America, 1988.

117. *Ministry Currents* (newsletter). Barna Research Group, 1992.

118. *Pastor-Parish Fit Instrument*. Washington, DC: Alban Institute.

119. Shawchuck, Norm. *How to Manage Conflict in the Church*. Indianapolis: Spiritual Resources, 1983.

120. *The Win Arn Report* (newsletter), Issue #36, 1992.